Help The Homeless

Off the Streets

One Person at a Time

Deacon Michael J. Oles

HTTP://WWW.OFFTHESTREETSNOW.COM

OFFTHESTREETSNOWSTARTUP@GMAIL.COM

A Not Forgotten Publication
Not.Forgotten.Publishing@gmail.com

"This book is awesome and has everything I look for and more as an avenue to teach how a heart changes, how God molds a person and uses them to do His will. It's a great introduction to OFF THE STREETS for people whom God has been speaking to about the homeless in our nation. It will help to facilitate movement in a stagnant world that doesn't know what to do with our friends the homeless." *Bill Wright, OTS Huntington Beach, CA*

"A fine telling of the OTS story." *George Stadler, OTS Lancaster*

"I am still continually inspired by what you have done—or rather, by what God has done through you. The book is excellent. It is very practical and gives people a concrete, step-by-step plan to build an OTS chapter in their city. I'm quite sure this will lead to many more homeless getting OFF THE STREETS!" *Fr. Joseph Gill, St. Mary Parish, Bethel, CT*

"I probably learned as much about you as a brother as I did about your work with the homeless. A well written, compelling story, and sure to help those who are looking at helping others in need." *Jack Oles, CMSAF (Ret.)*

"An inspirational story that needs to be shared, this book conveys a powerful message." *Deacon Kevin Moore, OTS Bridgeport, CT*

"Compelling, focused, and instructional—as well as heart pulling!" *Thomas Carr, OTS Lancaster, PA*

"What an inspirational story. I have no doubt this will be used as a primer for many communities around the country to help those in need." *Vince Oles, architect, Salt Lake City, UT*

"So inspiring. With the help of the Holy Spirit, OTS is already saving people and, God willing, will spread across the country." *Dorothy Hayes, Torrington, CT*

"Without your commitment and dedication to this effort we would not have moved as many households into permanent housing as we have in the past year. I commend you on your ease of process and the flexibility and speed at which this can happen. We thank you from the bottom of our hearts and pray that this teamwork continues on for as long as there are folks in need." *Doug Hopwood, Tabor Community Services, Lancaster, PA*

"Brought me to tears a few times and certainly convicted me to help the homeless even more. This book will be great to spread the OTS concept to other cities!" *Larry Burns, OTS Huntington Beach, CA*

"The idea behind OFF THE STREETS is such a simple one: that homeless people with a source of income can rapidly escape homelessness and get into a place of their own. We've turned this idea into a reality. We've found out what works and what does not work. We've built a good foundation, and now it's time for others who have received the calling to follow in our footsteps." *Joe Simons, OTS Danbury, CT*

"The narrative of the author's own faith journey has been merged nicely with the stories of those who are homeless. The Gospel theme of caring for the weak, the vulnerable, and the poor resonates throughout. What a powerful and beautiful ministry!" *Deacon Peter Jupin, St. John Neumann Catholic Church, Lancaster, PA*

"I will never forget how we were so discouraged in trying to find someone who could help us to meet the faces of the homeless. We had tried every organization but no one would help. It was at a lunch meeting that Deacon Mike Oles's name came to me like a bolt of lightning. I knew if I called him, he would be the one. I am grateful that we were able to meet so many of those who were helped to get OFF THE STREETS, to be safe and sound and finally comfortable." *Pat Postiglione, Director of Religious Education, Bridgeport, CT*

Contents

I never look at the masses as my responsibility.

I look at the individual. I can love only one person at a time.
I can feed only one person at a time.

Just one, one, one.

You get closer to Christ by coming closer to each other. As Jesus
said, "Whatever you do to the least of my brethren, you do to me."

So you begin . . . I begin.

I picked up one person—

maybe if I didn't pick up that one person
I wouldn't have picked up 42,000.

The whole work is only a drop in the ocean. But
if I didn't put the drop in, the ocean would be one drop less.

Same thing for you.
Same thing for your family.
Same thing in the church where you go.

Just begin . . . one, one, one.

Mother Teresa
Words to Love By, p. 79

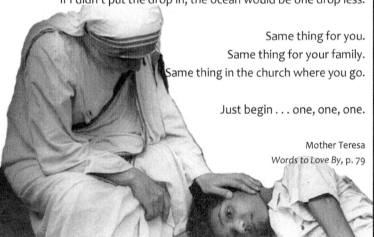

One Person at a Time

WHAT IS THE FIRST THING that comes to mind when you hear the words *homeless person?*

Answers I've heard have included "without a home," "hungry," "dirty." We tend to consider the plight of the homeless to be something they have done to themselves. They must have made some wrong decisions, terrible decisions. When we see someone begging for money or sleeping on a park bench, without thinking we might say, "Why doesn't he get a job? Why doesn't he clean himself up? That lazy so and so, he's a drain on society." We might even say, as the soldiers and Jewish leaders said of Jesus when he was hanging on the cross, "Let him save himself."

> **What is our responsibility for people who are homeless? Jesus commands us to see his own face in every person we meet.**

Such judgments fail to see the face of Christ in the terrible indignity of homelessness. They are judgments that Pope Francis cautions us not to make:

> How can it be that it is not a news item when an elderly homeless person dies of exposure,

but it is news when the stock market loses two points? (*Evangelii Gaudium*, 53)

Many of the homeless are in fact invisible to us. They don't dress themselves and their children in ragged, dirty clothes, because if they did, other people would avoid eye contact, make snide remarks, and cast judgment. Instead, they try their best to fit in.

So, what is our responsibility for people who are homeless? Jesus commands us to see His own face in every person we meet—not in a broad-brush way that dulls our senses, but in the individual we see before us.

This book introduces one way that people in Connecticut, Pennsylvania, and California are already helping individual persons and families move OFF THE STREETS and into homes of their own. We share our story with the hope that, when you see how easy it is, you will be inspired to start a chapter of OFF THE STREETS in your state, in your community.

If you are unable to start your own chapter but would still like to support the mission of OTS, please send a check made payable to OFF THE STREETS to the following address, and please tell us that you learned about our mission from this book:

OFF THE STREETS
PO Box 591
Bethel CT 06801

It typically takes about $500 to move one person or family OFF THE STREETS. All donations are tax deductible.

God bless you!

Hungry not only for bread—
but hungry for love.

Naked not only for clothing—
but naked of human dignity and respect.

Homeless not only for want of a room of bricks—
but homeless because of rejection.

Mother Teresa, *Words to Love By*

"For I was hungry and you gave me food,

I was thirsty and you gave me drink,

a stranger and you welcomed me."

Matthew 25:35

What Is OFF THE STREETS?

OFF THE STREETS (OTS) IS a 501(c)(3) nonprofit charitable organization registered with the IRS and with the states of Connecticut, Pennsylvania, and California—so far. Its mission is to provide a security deposit and basic furniture and living needs for those homeless people who have no other means of providing these but do have a means of paying a monthly rent. The homeless person finds a place he or she can afford. OTS then pays the security deposit directly to the landlord. (Repayment is not expected but, when it occurs, the money is used to pay other security deposits.) No government funding is taken. There are no paid staff, no professional fundraisers, no offices, and no utilities to pay. All furniture and other living needs are donated.

Since 2009, OFF THE STREETS has helped more than four hundred individuals and families to move into homes of their own

OTS was started as a faith-based organization by a Roman Catholic deacon, members of the parish he served, and members of other Christian churches in the community (one of the founding members of the board of directors was a member of the First Congregational Church of Danbury, and a local Methodist church allows OTS to use its parking lot to collect donations and provides space in its basement for storage). This faith-based approach is reflected in this book. Such motivation is not, however, a requirement. We are fortunate to have developed a fast and effective way to get people with a source of income out of homelessness and into housing. Your motivation may be different, yet the result can be the same: people moved quickly OFF THE STREETS and into homes of their own.

"Christ came to us as an individual human being, and during His life on Earth He approached us as individual human beings. He didn't wave his hand over the crowds and heal all the sick among them. Instead, He healed individual persons as they came to Him, and still does. So, when He commands us (in John 15:12) to love one another as He has loved us, isn't this what He means?"

Alice S. Morrow Rowan

Who Are the Homeless?

HOMELESS PEOPLE ARE men, women, and children who do not have a house, apartment, or room to call home and instead spend their nights sleeping in public areas (such as on a street or in a park), in a car, or in a shelter operated by a church or other community organization.

> "The land will never lack for needy persons; that is why I command you: 'Open your hand freely to your poor and to your needy kin in your land.'"
>
> Deuteronomy 15:11

Why does a person or family become homeless? It is often assumed that the cause is mental illness or addiction or both. This is certainly true in some cases. According to a December 2013 report by the U.S. Conference of Mayors, "on average, 30 percent of homeless adults are severely mentally ill."[1] And according to the National Alliance to End Homelessness, "on a given night in 2012, nearly 40 percent of the homeless population had serious mental illness or conditions related to chronic substance abuse."[2] The National Coalition for the Homeless points out that "many people who are addicted to alcohol and drugs never become homeless," so clearly these problems alone

[1] http://www.usmayors.org/pressreleases/uploads/2013/1210-report-HH.pdf
[2] http://www.endhomelessness.org/pages/mental_physical_health

are not necessarily the reason that people are homeless, though "people who are poor and addicted are clearly at increased risk."[3] The National Alliance to End Homelessness notes that "mental and physical health problems [are] exacerbated by living on the streets and in shelters," and it acknowledges that substance use is "prevalent among homeless populations."[4] The main reason for homelessness, however, is the inability to find affordable housing.[5]

Every situation is unique. One person, for one reason or another (such as losing her job or encountering unexpected medical expenses), falls behind in her rent and is evicted. Another person has been living in an abusive relationship and gets thrown out or finally leaves. People have scraped together money for a deposit but then have been fleeced by the landlord. They may not have a good grasp of the English language or know what their legal rights are, so they don't know how to get help.

Even when a homeless person has a regular source of income (such as a job or social security payments) and can find an affordable place to live, he or she often has no resources for paying a security deposit and furnishing a home. Available income, instead of being saved, is often used to pay for a motel room in order to avoid staying in a shelter. It is also common to give one's money away, in response to pressure from other homeless persons, out of empathy at the plight of those who have no income, and out of a sense of hopelessness about their own ability to ever save enough. By paying the security deposit and providing home furnishings, OTS closes this gap in resources, and opens the door to new opportunities.

---

[3] http://nationalhomeless.org/about-homelessness
[4] http://www.endhomelessness.org/pages/faqs#why
[5] http://www.endhomelessness.org/pages/faqs#why

Seven Myths About Homeless People[6]

Myth 1: All homeless people sleep on the streets or in shelters.
Reality: At least 30 percent live in a vehicle.

Myth 2: Homelessness is always related to mental illness and/or substance abuse.
Reality: It is more often due to economic hardship than to any other issue.

Myth 3: Homeless individuals are fine with being homeless.
Reality: Many consider themselves to be between homes in the same way as unemployed people consider themselves to be between jobs.

Myth 4: The homeless don't take care of themselves.
Reality: A growing number of men and women "wake up on the street or in a shelter, get dressed, and head to work."[7] Many others spend their days looking for work. They do whatever it takes not to appear homeless.

Myth 5: The homeless want only money and food.
Reality: Most want help getting off the street and back on their feet.

Myth 6: Humans are the only homeless who need help.
Reality: From 5 to 24 percent of homeless people have pets, who need help too.[8]

Myth 7: The homeless don't use the Internet.
Reality: Many of the homeless have a cell phone and/or some kind of portable computer. "It's their lifeline to civilization."[9] Free Wi-Fi is available in many locations.

---

[6] Adapted from "7 Myths About Homeless People Debunked," by Ann Brenoff, *Huffington Post*, May 3, 2014, http://www.huffingtonpost.com/2014/05/03/7-things-homeless-people-not-true_n_5206475.html?utm_hp_ref=impact&ncid=fcbklnkushpmg00000010

[7] Ronan Farrow on MSNBC's *TODAY* show, March 24, 2014, http://www.today.com/video/today/54761848#54761848

[8] For more on the homeless and pets, see http://www.petsofthehomeless.org/what-we-do/faqs.html

[9] Ann Brenoff, *Huffington Post*.

"Jesus spoke to them, 'Take courage, it is I; do not be afraid.' Peter said in reply, 'Lord, if it is you, command me to come to you on the water.' He said, 'Come.' Peter got out of the boat and began to walk on the water toward Jesus." *Matthew 14:27–29*

Stepping Out of the Boat

YOU ARE READING THIS BOOK, so your mind and heart must at least be open to doing something—or something more—to help those who are homeless. Maybe you haven't taken the first step yet, because you are still wrestling with your own attitude toward the homeless, or maybe for one reason or another you're afraid. Maybe you've already been trying to make a difference—volunteering at a soup kitchen or shelter, or donating money to these and other organizations that serve the homeless—but have grown frustrated or even angry at what seems like a never-ending, closed cycle for many of the individuals you have encountered. In any case, it takes great courage to step out of the safety of the boat and have an encounter with Jesus on the water.

I've been there—resistant, fearful, trying, frustrated, angry—and so have the other OTS team members who have shared their stories in the testimonials section of this book (see pages 49–78). In the next few chapters, I share some of the journey by which the Holy Spirit brought me to start the first chapter of OFF THE STREETS. I tell my story not because it's about me but because, as St. Paul says in Romans 15:18–19, "I will not venture to speak of anything except what Christ has accomplished through me . . . by the power of the Spirit of God."

The Thrill of the Chase

I GREW UP IN A TRADITIONAL ROMAN CATHOLIC FAMILY. My parents and grandparents were very devout, and much of our life was centered around the Church. My parents told us we were "upper middle class," and we believed it, even though they worked hard to put us through Catholic schools and universities. They never lectured us about helping others in need, they just showed us by their example.

> I became totally fascinated by the idea of mankind pushing the limits of knowledge. . . .
> I was looking for a new adventure. Every job had to be more exciting than the last one.

I went to Catholic grammar school in Torrington, Connecticut, then to public high school, then to Fairfield University, a Jesuit school, where I majored in physics. In those days, there was no social outreach or community action requirement in the curriculum, as there is on many campuses today, but we were taught that we had been made in God's image and we were stretched to the limits, in philosophy, ethics, and theology classes, to use our God-given talents. These classes were as much the core of my coursework as mastering partial differential equations and nuclear science.

Hardly a moment after I graduated from Fairfield, in 1964, Uncle Sam came knocking at the door wanting to draft me into the Army. I decided to apply to the Air Force Officer Training School instead. I was admitted, and became a second lieutenant. Within a year I was offered the opportunity to work with NASA on the Apollo lunar landing mission at the Manned Spacecraft Center (now the Lyndon B. Johnson Space Center) in Houston, Texas. It was in this position that I became totally fascinated by the idea of mankind pushing the limits of knowledge. At twenty-two, I was now working in the same office as the world's most brilliant mathematicians and scientists, determining spacecraft flight trajectories and orbits with slide rules, mechanical calculators, and massive computers.

From NASA I went to the Advanced Research Projects Agency (which carries out defense-related research and development projects), where conceptual thinking was the norm and our only limitation was how far our imaginations could take us, but the probability of success was maybe 10 percent. There was no shame in failure—only in not trying. That way of thinking is perhaps what shaped my future.

In every assignment I took in the Air Force, I was looking for a new adventure. Every job had to be more exciting than the last one. But after twenty years, I decided I didn't want to be a "staffer" or part of the Washington crowd. I realized I would never feel satisfaction from becoming part of the "upper crust." I found myself longing for my earlier assignments, the grassroots stuff. In 1984 I retired as a lieutenant colonel and made a sideways move into the civilian defense industry. There, I thought, I would find satisfaction; there I could concentrate on profit and loss.

My first few jobs, with Norden Systems, Perkin-Elmer, Hughes, and Raytheon, were indeed exciting. I had already earned a master's degree in systems management and become a program manager. But after fourteen years, it became clear that climbing the corporate ladder was no more satisfying than climbing the ranks in the military. I wasn't cut out for it. When in 1998 I was laid off from Raytheon, I launched my third career, as a high school physics teacher—a career that proved to be unimaginably hard, not at all what I'd expected (I loved physics but found I didn't have the patience to deal with indifferent high schoolers who didn't share that passion), and therefore lasted only a few years.

As all of this was going on, other things were happening. In 1966 I married the love of my life, Kathleen Schultz. We had met at a Fairfield University mixer. On a dare from my buddies, I asked her to dance. The rest, as the saying goes, is history. Over the years our family grew by four children (who eventually gave us ten grandchildren). When I retired from the Air Force in 1984, we returned to our home state, Connecticut, and settled in the town of Bethel.

> **I began to think I wanted to become a deacon. . . . I didn't even really know why. Something was gnawing at me.**

While I was working at Raytheon, I began to think I wanted to become a deacon. I told my pastor, naively assuming that he could just appoint me. At that point I didn't even really know why. Something was gnawing at me. Maybe it was pride. Maybe I wanted the prestige. In any case, I was selected to begin four years of formation in 1998. Shortly after, I was laid off from Raytheon. Those four years were very difficult. I was struggling to teach physics to high schoolers, and the studies I was required to undertake to become a deacon were intense—nearly the equivalent of working toward a master's degree in religious studies.

When I was ordained in 2002 and assigned to St. Mary's parish in Bethel, I told Kathy I was done with teaching, done with the secular life. I was going to be a deacon. Kathy said, "What are you going to do with your time? You'll be bored to death." My response was, "I don't know what God's plan is for me, but I'll let Him help me figure it out."

The first two years were like an extended vacation. I came and went as I wanted, did a lot of bicycling, and went to the beach in the summer. I also did a lot of scuba diving. I was particularly fascinated by this pastime: feeling weightless and moving effortlessly through the sparkling water, climbing underwater walls with ease, seeing all the varieties of God's sea creatures—the turtles, sharks, and shimmering fish. Now, I thought, I have achieved fulfillment! So I went gallivanting around the world in search of the perfect dive site.

Slowly the thrill wore off. Every dive was in pursuit of that special moment—which almost never came. I can still recall one day, in the beautiful waters of the Caribbean, saying to myself, *Is this all there is: wondering what the underwater visibility will be today? There's got to be more to life than this.* I was smart enough to be a physicist, but my intellect was also my Achilles heel. I was thinking as man does, not as God does.

Back in 1984, soon after my retirement from the Air Force and our return to Connecticut, I had attended an ecumenical service at another church in the Danbury area. A guest speaker, Dr. Paul Hines, spoke to us about the Dorothy Day Hospitality House, a homeless shelter he had helped to found in Danbury a couple of years earlier. He was looking for volunteers to stay overnight one night per month. OK, I thought, I'll help. Naively I signed up.

I had no idea what I was getting into.

I had associated with the most advanced scientists and engineers, and with leaders of companies, all of whom were financially successful, a few of whom were even very wealthy. But the homeless? I'd never met them. I'd known poverty as a kid, but homelessness? No. Never! The homeless and homelessness were off my radar screen.

The first few times I stayed at the shelter in Danbury were nightmares for me. The shelter is a big open room with seventeen twin beds separated by partitions. There's almost no privacy—just a tiny bathroom for men and another for women, and a shower room, which also serves as a place to do laundry. There is heat in the winter, but no air conditioning in the summer, just a few fans. There's no TV or radio. There's no place to hide your stuff, including valuables such as wallets and keys, from roving eyes. Each person's stuff is his or her own responsibility. The odors in the shelter are often difficult to stomach; anyone who has walked around in wet or humid weather knows, for example, what it's like to take those shoes off. Trying to sleep at the shelter was unnerving, with the phone ringing, people knocking on the door in the middle of the night and wanting to come in, and guests snoring and wandering back and forth to the bathroom or to get a drink of water or just unable to sleep. Every time I stayed at the shelter I was fearful, so every night I spent there was an act of faith.

While I was still working in the defense industry and volunteering just one night each month, I would arrange

> **Naively I signed up. I had no idea what I was getting into. . . . The homeless and homelessness were off my radar screen.**

to start work late the day after staying overnight at the shelter so I'd have time to get myself together. When I was teaching, I would volunteer only on a Friday or Saturday night. Many a time I would cancel, using every excuse in the book not to go, because I was just plain scared. Finally one of the coordinators, who opened up the shelter each night, said to me, "Mike, you've got to decide what to do. You can't keep signing up and then backing out. It's putting a big strain on the rest of us." It was a hard ministry, and I wasn't really strong enough for it. But something kept luring me back.

In about 1990, one of the four coordinators moved to Ireland, leaving a void in the shelter's all-volunteer staff. My record was spotty, and showing up continued to be a battle for me, but for some strange, unknown reason, I stepped up to the plate. "I'll do it," I said. I thus went from staying with the homeless one night a month to staying with them seven nights in a row every fourth week. The strange, unknown reason wasn't reason at all; it was faith—though I didn't quite realize that yet.

From the beginning I had viewed the homeless as the unfortunate ones whom I was helping. I often put myself on a pedestal: I was God's gift to them. They were the ne'er-do-wells, the ones wasting their lives, not doing all they could to get themselves out of their situation.

Every night that I went to the shelter, I punched an imaginary card for performing a charitable service for the guests, and I just knew my sacrifice of time and energy and fear would be compensated when I reached the Pearly Gates and St. Peter asked, "So, Oles, what did you do with your life?" I was, in other words, concerned primarily with myself.

At one point after I was ordained a deacon, I was asked to conduct a world religions class. The other volunteer at the shelter that night was a Unitarian. Thinking I was preparing for the class, I asked him what the Unitarians were all about—what did they believe and what were their practices?

"Hard to say, Mike," he replied.

I pressed him: "How about belief in God, for starters?"

"Some Unitarians believe in God," he said. "But some are agnostic, and some are really atheists."

"You can't be serious."

"I'm deadly serious," he replied. Then I asked him, "Why do you come here?"

He threw the question back at me. "Why do you?"

I told him about my imaginary card.

He looked at me as though I were an alien from another planet. "What?"

"So that when I reach the Pearly Gates I can show Saint Peter what I did with my life. Your turn: Why do you Unitarians do it?"

"It's not so easy."

"Humor me."

"Well, we do it as an end in itself."

"Huh?"

"We do it because it's the right thing to do. It's an end in itself."

It was as if he had jolted me with a cattle prod. While I was looking for the payoff for myself, this man—who might not even believe in God—was being a better Christian than I was.

Eventually I was to be jolted again, and again, as the following two stories illustrate.

The Transfiguration

THE MANY NIGHTS I SPENT at the Dorothy Day House as a volunteer and coordinator were always difficult for me. I felt uneasy and afraid, and I really couldn't believe that people were able to survive by living that way.

> I saw him as Bartimaeus, the blind man in Mark 10:46–52, but instead of reaching out to be healed of his blindness, he continued to go his own way.

Over the years I got to know many of the guests. One of them upset me more than any of the others. His name was Michael Kusen.

Mike was a Vietnam veteran and had been homeless for many years. His appearance never changed: he always had his Vietnam hat on, and his clothes were always scraggly, filthy, unkempt. He looked exactly like the stereotypical homeless person you might see on the streets of New York or on TV or in the movies.

I always felt that Mike was an intelligent fellow and I was very angry that he was at the shelter. I scolded him many a time, accusing him of wasting his life, his God-given talents, and my time. He never followed through on any appointments I made for him at the Veterans Administration. I saw him as Bartimaeus, the blind man in Mark 10:46–52, but instead of reaching out to be healed of his blindness, he continued to go his own way.

There were few options for the homeless in Danbury. The winters can be brutal, and one February it was. We'd already had a lot of snow, and it was icy everywhere, and windy. Just getting out of the car and walking to the house or the office was painful. I was scheduled to open the shelter as coordinator each night that week. There is never a great time to be coordinator, but that week it was particularly frustrating. There was literally no other place to send anyone who could not get into the shelter. The coordinator had to make on-the-spot decisions as to who got in, knowing that each person who didn't was going to be spending a miserable night out in the cold.

The people were so numb they literally couldn't feel the tickets being put into their hands and I would pinch their fingers together so they could hold on to them. . . . In the midst of these miserable people stood Mike Kusen.

I recall that week as though it were yesterday. The shelter opened at 9:00 P.M. The homeless would gather around the doors, waiting sometimes two hours in the pitch black for them to open. When I showed up that Monday night, I was met by a docile crowd. They talked in hushed tones, too cold to raise their voices. There were maybe twenty-five people waiting for a chance to spend the night in one of the shelter's sixteen beds.

Our solution at that time was to hold a lottery. That night when I gave out the tickets, the people were so numb they literally couldn't feel the tickets being put into their hands and I would pinch their fingers together so they could hold on to them. There was muffled grumbling, and a little jostling for position, as if that would make a difference. In the midst of these miserable people stood Mike Kusen. As usual, I felt angry that he was even there. As much as I wanted him to begin to do something good with his life, I always failed to convince him.

I proceeded to call out the lottery numbers by the last three digits on the stubs: 923 . . . 918 . . . 903 . . . 914 . . . and

so on. I couldn't bear to look at the people; my heart was broken. Each time I said a number, a person would step forward and I'd check their ticket and let them in. Sometimes they didn't react immediately, so I gave them a second chance by calling out the number again. After a third time, I gave up and moved on to the next number. After getting sixteen people inside, I had to send seven or eight others off into the miserable cold. May God have mercy on my soul.

Tuesday night was a repeat of Monday night. Twenty-five souls were waiting, with Mike Kusen in their midst. I called out the lottery numbers. Mike didn't get in, and I distinctly remember him saying as I sent him away, "I can't believe it. Two nights in a row."

Wednesday night was the same, except this time I was able to see Mike Kusen not as a faceless, miserable soul but as a human being suffering and near death. As I called out the lottery numbers, I thought, if Mike doesn't get in, I'd better get him to the hospital; he looks really bad. But again he didn't get in, and after I assigned beds to the sixteen who did make it in, I went outside to look for Mike, but he had disappeared into the horrible inky black of the streets and alleys.

During the day on Thursday I couldn't function at my job. My mind kept focusing on the lot of the homeless—and on what a great sacrifice I would be making to be at the shelter again that night. At the same time, my stomach was in knots knowing that I would also be turning people back out into hopelessness. It was another brutal, windy, icy day. It was God-awful just getting from the office to my car.

On my way to the shelter that night, my thoughts shifted from the anticipated mass of humanity I knew I would meet there and focused in on Mike Kusen. I was hoping against hope that he would not be at the shelter that night. But as I walked past the crowd to open the doors, there he was. He was ashen blue, a standing corpse, a shell of a man. A thought crossed my mind as I entered the shelter to get the lottery tickets: I'll fake the lottery tonight to ensure that Mike gets in. I was ready to do just that when another inner voice interrupted me: "You'll do no such thing!" I didn't argue with that voice, and complied with its firm command.

I proceeded to pass out the lottery tickets. My heart was aching. There were so many people and, as usual, not enough beds. When I handed a ticket to Mike, I whispered a prayer: "Dear God, in your mercy, please choose Mike to stay tonight."

I called out the numbers: 758 . . . 763 . . . 744 . . . and so on. And then I called a number and Mike Kusen stepped forward. I was so thankful to God that for a moment I forgot about the misery of those I was about to send away.

But I did send them away. And there I was, in the warmth of the shelter, assigning beds, and feeling pretty darn good. I hadn't faked the lottery and, thanks be to God, Mike Kusen had made it in! I was almost laughing.

I looked at Mike, this miserable person who had wasted his life, who was a complete failure, and what I saw nearly took my breath away.

And then there was a tap on my shoulder. At first I didn't pay attention. But then I was shoved. I turned to look, and it was Mike Kusen, holding his lottery ticket. If a person could be dead and standing up—that's what I'd like you to experience in your mind.

He stretched out his hand with the lottery ticket in it and said to me matter-of-factly, "I'm giving up my bed." He looked like I could knock him over with a feather.

"Michael, you're delirious. Take your bed."

He looked me right in the eye and said in a very authoritative voice, "I'm giving up my bed."

"To who?" I retorted.

"I don't know. She's outside," Mike replied.

"What are you talking about? Where are you going to sleep tonight?"

"I'll be on the streets," he said, "but I think she needs the bed more than I do."

Mike now had my full attention. I followed him outside. There was no one there. I said to Mike, "Let's go back in."

"No. Look over there."

"There's no one there," I said as he pushed me toward the edge of the parking lot. Then he pointed down at what looked to me like a plastic bag of garbage. As I examined it further, I could see the outline of a woman. Then I could see her face. I'd never seen her before. I asked her, "Do you know this man?"

Mike Kusen wasn't the blind man— I was.

"No," she murmured.

I asked Mike, "Do you know her?"

He said, "No. Today is the first time I've seen her. I think she's new to Danbury."

I looked at Mike, this miserable person who had wasted his life, who was a complete failure, and what I saw nearly took my breath away: I saw the face of God. It was as if he was transfigured before my very eyes: the suffering, self-less Christ in my midst.

Mike was doing something that was beyond my comprehension, beyond my ability to absorb. Here was a person I'd looked at for many years as a wasted life, yet he was doing something I could barely begin to grasp. This man was looking beyond himself and seeing another human being who he felt was suffering beyond his suffering, and offering her the only thing he had in his possession—his lottery ticket; he was taking his one opportunity to get out of the misery of that night and giving it away to a perfect stranger.

All those years I'd been going to the shelter thinking how generous I was, helping others in need and looking for payback at the Pearly Gates, believing I was a good man. But on that cold, miserable night, my life changed forever. Mike Kusen had done something that had shaken my soul to the quick. It was a wake-up call from the Holy Spirit, telling me how foolish I was to think I was offering something to the destitute. Mike Kusen wasn't the blind man—I was, and God was telling me that if I searched deeply enough, I could see the face of Christ in another human being. Christ is all around us, but the Holy Spirit had to smack me in the face with Mike Kusen in order for me to begin to realize that.

I began to look at Mike as my closest, dearest friend. If he would give up his life for a perfect stranger, how much more could I rely on him if my life depended on it? Never again could I look at a person and not ache to see the face of Christ as I had that fateful night in Danbury, Connecticut, when God opened my eyes through his instrument, a homeless man named Michael Kusen.

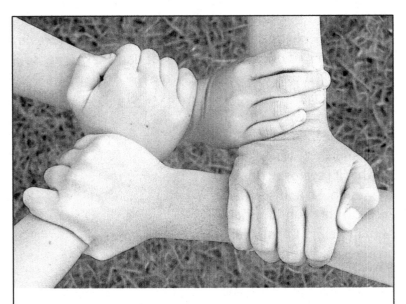

"The four-hand seat carry is used to carry a conscious casualty who can help support himself while he is being carried. . . . The [two] bearers' forearms form the seat."

From http://www.armystudyguide.com

The Power of Two

I WAS INVITED BY PAT, a director of religious education, to speak to some eighth graders about homelessness. I brought along a homeless man, Al, who was willing to speak to this group of young people about his life. Neither he nor I had any idea what to expect, and he was clearly nervous.

> How attentive and interested the students had been. We thought that was the end of it. But it was only the beginning.

The students asked Al many questions during the hour we were with them, and he responded with remarkably personal and frank comments about what it's like to live on the streets. Afterward, as we drove back to the shelter, both he and I expressed amazement at how attentive and interested the students had been. We thought that was the end of it.

But it was only the beginning. A few weeks later Pat called me. The students, she said, had been very moved by Al's description of life on the streets and they wanted to help. She asked if I would bring Al back again. When we met with them the second time, the students handed me a check for $750 they had raised. They wanted me to use it to help Al get into a home of his own. Both Al and I were dumbstruck.

I brought the check home and placed it on my dresser. It sat there for a week or two, until Pat called me again.

The students wanted to know if I'd gotten Al a home yet. I hadn't done anything. What could I do? For years I'd tried to encourage the homeless people I'd meet to get out of the shelter, but my words seemed to fall mostly on deaf ears. To me the homeless seemed hopeless.

A week later Pat called again. Of course I had done nothing. By the fourth phone call I was almost afraid to answer the phone.

I realized I had to do something, anything, to get Pat and those students off my back. I wasn't motivated by Al, the homeless person. It was those persistent students who were driving me out of my mind. At night I would dream they were calling me and break out in a cold sweat. These kids were literally forcing me, a deacon, to take action.

It doesn't take a rocket scientist to change the lives of the homeless. It does take the power of two: an idealistic child not yet jaded by pessimism, doubt, and cynicism, guided by the Holy Spirit.

In desperation, I finally told Al that if he found a place to live and a way to pay the monthly rent, I would use the money the students had raised to pay the security deposit and to buy some furniture to help him get started. The result felt like a miracle: he was soon living in a home he could call his own.

Not long afterward, I got a phone call from another director of religious education. She had been talking to Pat and she asked if I would come talk to her students. I went, and again, after hearing a homeless person's story, the kids raised money, then turned it over to me to use to get the homeless person OFF THE STREETS. The same thing happened eight or nine times over the next three years as students from four parishes made it possible for twelve homeless persons to move into homes of their own after years of living on the streets. Still, I didn't get the message.

The Thrill of the Faith

FINALLY I STARTED THINKING, maybe I could start a nonprofit. But I had no idea what to do next. I'd been involved in only very large organizations—the Air Force, the aerospace industry, the public school system, and the Roman Catholic Church. I looked at a 501(c)(3) nonprofit application. It was intimidating. I built up this great big wall between me and making it happen. I thought, well, I've got to get a staff, I've got to get money, somehow I've got to come up with funding, I'll have to pay for a receptionist, for an office—where will all that money come from? I kept delaying and delaying and delaying. Meanwhile, the Holy Spirit kept smacking me across the head: Look, if these kids can do something, why can't you as an adult do something more? But I was firmly grounded in reason, with barely a lick of real faith.

> **The Holy Spirit kept smacking me across the head: Look, if these kids can do something, why can't you as an adult do something more?**

Then I found out I had prostate cancer, and one day I was nursing a couple of margaritas down at the Mexican restaurant when it dawned on me that I might not live that long and the time to move was now. So I found Attorney William Hagan and Bob Kozlowski, a CPA. I told them what I wanted to do and that I didn't have any money to do it.

We met several times and within a couple of weeks, OFF THE STREETS was launched (a suitable rocket-science word). For the board of directors I recruited individuals who I knew had a link with the homeless. Other rocket-science terms could be used to describe the first couple of years: *false starts, mission creep, flameout, crash and burn, disorientation, wasted resources, midcourse corrections, failure to communicate.* It really was the Holy Spirit who held us together through chaos—chaos often caused by me. Four years later, all but two original board members remain.[10]

---

[10] Members of the Danbury team, from left to right: Larry Havey, Nick Santarelli, Thomas Levesque, Joe Simons, Rich Schlemmer, Sean Payne, Ann Leiss, and Joan Finn.

Christ continues to bleed and weep and
cry out, "Why have you abandoned me?" . . .

Whatever you do to the least of these, he said,
you do to me. . . .

We encounter him on the subway, step over him on the
sidewalk, and go out of our way to avoid him when
we feel like he might make demands on our time.

. . . We see Jesus every day, read about him
in the papers, hear about him on the news.

He is everywhere there is someone who is small,
or neglected, or disrespected, or discarded.

He is with the unloved, the bullied and abused. . .

We are called to be heralds of Christ—
to celebrate him the way they did
that day in Jerusalem. . . .

These palms challenge us not to
step over him, or ignore him.
And they challenge us
to remember
not only what we
have done to him,
but also what   Look
he has done   to these palms.
for us. . .   Look at what
we are called to do
—and who we are
called to be.

Fr. Michael Letteer, Palm Sunday 2014,
St. John Neumann Church, Lancaster, PA

Have You Ever Thought?

by Tom Greco and His Students at St. Thomas the Apostle Church, Norwalk, Connecticut

Have you ever thought about the rich and the poor?
How different they live. How different they are.
What do they live in? Have you ever wondered how
some people go from mansions to houses,
or from houses to boxes?

Have you ever thought about the rich and the poor?
The haves and the have nots? I know I haven't!
I come across homeless every day.
Some are collecting cans,
some are begging for change,
some are wondering how
to put their lives back together.

Although I see these types of people daily,
I don't stop to help. I don't stop to give.
I just don't stop. After all,
this is just human nature, isn't it? . . .
It's a dog eat dog world out there.

While the world may often be an uncaring place,
we don't have to be uncaring people.
All it takes is some sharing, some caring,
and some compassion.
If we all shared, if we all cared,
if we all showed some compassion,
imagine what the world would be like!
I think people should share.
Many have much more than they know, or realize.
They have things in their closets that they
no longer wear or need, or just don't like.

Why can't we just share?
Why can't we just give to the poor?

If you would like to see such people in need,
just jump in the car and take a short ride
to any homeless shelter, such as
Dorothy Day House in Danbury
and countless others.
You may not even have to go that far.
Just look down the street.
You may catch a glimpse of any number of them
collecting bottles and cans to survive.

Some people have 72-inch plasma TVs
while others have no food.
Some people have two billion dollars
while for others $2 is like having a billion!
Some live in apartments which are like
penthouses to them,
while others spread out their cardboard box
on the cold concrete for comfort.

Imagine what could happen if we pictured ourselves
living on the street—no home, no money
—nothing but the clothes on our back.
It's pretty sad, don't you think?

If you think as we do, then lend a hand,
share your heart, and give just a little
to someone for whom a little is a whole lot!
That's the difference between the rich and the poor.

Have you thought about how rich you are?
Can you give to someone
who is among the have nots?

"After praying the Angelus with faithful gathered in St. Peter's Square on the fourth Sunday of Advent 2013, Pope Francis spoke of the great difficulties that families without fixed dwelling face—not unlike the Holy Family, to whom the Lord Jesus was born in a barn, and that experienced forced flight from their native land into Egypt. 'Family and home go together,' said Pope Francis. He went on to say, 'I call on everyone—individuals, organs of society, authorities—to do everything possible to assure that every family has a place to live.' "

From www.news.va, Official Vatican Network

The Next Chapter

IN SEPTEMBER 2012, Kathleen and I moved from Connecticut to Lancaster, Pennsylvania. Naturally, for the first few months we were focused on settling into our new home and meeting our new parish family at St. John Neumann. During that time my thoughts were seldom on the homeless. But within three months, the Spirit was stirring me to take action.

> **It was intimidating to see that so many organizations were already helping the homeless in one way or another. . . . It would be easy to walk away and feel justified. But I couldn't.**

I learned that members of our parish were involved with a Friday evening meal served at historic St. Mary's Church in Lancaster. I thought about going to help out, and one snowy day I did just that. It was as if I'd never left Danbury. I showed up before the evening meal was served. I conversed with others who were waiting to enter. I quickly found at least three or four persons among this group of perhaps twenty who admitted to being homeless.

The door opened and a greeter welcomed us into the small dining room as he brushed the snow off our coats. I sat with the guests and many told me they were homeless. Some had a job, others had another source of money such as unemployment or social security income. A few wanted

---

to know why I was asking them questions, but overall they were willing to speak to me, a stranger in their midst.

I got home from that meal believing that there was certainly a need for OTS in Lancaster. I mentioned this to Kathleen. She was immediately emphatic about what I could and couldn't do. She knew my passion for the homeless. She knew I could easily become as immersed in Lancaster as I had been for twenty-five years in Danbury. "Enough," she said. "You've done enough. It's time to pass on this work to someone else. You cannot run an OTS in Lancaster like you did in Connecticut. You can be an advisor, but that's it!"

"OK," I said.

I was invited to talk with a group of representatives of the organizations that were already serving Lancaster's homeless population.

Soon after, I visited the day shelter run by Lancaster's Water Street Ministries, where the homeless can go to get out of the elements, shower, do laundry, make phone calls, receive mail, and learn about a wide range of other services designed to help them. In my exuberance, I blurted out to one of the staff members who I was and that I was considering starting an OTS chapter in Lancaster. The staff member pointed to two very long tables covered with brochures and fliers filled with information about the many homeless services already provided in Lancaster.

This could have been the end of my venture to start a Lancaster chapter of OTS. It was intimidating to see that so many organizations were already helping the homeless in one way or another. It was also, and still is, wonderful to see this small city's very large heart for the disenfranchised in society. It would be easy to walk away and feel justified.

But I couldn't. I knew I was still being called to do something, but I had no idea how to proceed. I was really struggling. I made a few false starts. But I quickly realized that the paradigm, the formula, that we had used in Danbury, of responding directly to the individuals I met at the shelter, wouldn't work in Lancaster. Another approach was needed.

I was invited to talk with a group of representatives of the organizations that were already serving Lancaster's homeless population. At this meeting, it became clear that together these organizations had in place systems and professional staff prepared to assess the needs and resources of their homeless clients. When they determined that an individual or family needed and was in a position to accept the assistance that OTS could provide, they would contact us and we would leap into action.

> **Together these organizations had in place systems and professional staff prepared to assess the needs and resources of their homeless clients.**

By the time we reached this point, I had already gotten the ball rolling to involve the parishioners of St. John Neumann in starting a Lancaster OTS. I knew that coming in all fired up with another "new program" could easily backfire. I'd already experienced and could understand the skepticism of the folks at the Water Street day center, who had seen many an impostor try to take advantage of the homeless in one way or another. I took courage from the fact that I'd been in the parish for a few months and people were getting to know me. When I brought the idea to the pastor, Monsignor Richard Youtz, he was very much in favor and even agreed to be the group's spiritual advisor.

Now that I had a green light, I reserved the church's library for an evening informational meeting a few weeks out. For a couple of weeks prior to the meeting I put an announcement in the bulletin describing OTS and inviting parishioners to the meeting. On the weekend before, I spoke about OTS and the upcoming meeting at the Saturday evening and Sunday Masses.

There was one more piece to set in place. The key factor in the birth of OTS was putting an actual face on the concept of homelessness. I approached a man and woman I'd met at the day center, a couple on a very limited income who had been in and out of homelessness for years. When they had a little money they would stay at a motel; when the money was exhausted, they would stay at the shelters. I invited them to come and speak at this introductory meeting. They agreed.

> **The key factor in the birth of OFF THE STREETS was putting an actual face on the concept of homelessness.**

The meeting was scheduled to take place in the church's library, which could comfortably hold up to a dozen people. Until a few minutes before the meeting was to begin, this space looked to be more than adequate. By 7:00 we had exceeded this capacity. Fortunately the meeting hall was available that evening, so we moved into that much larger room. By the time everyone had arrived, there were more than thirty of us present.

OTS Lancaster moved its first person into housing in July 2013. In its first year it settled more than eighty persons into new homes. A third chapter was started in Bridgeport, Connecticut, and a fourth chapter in Huntington Beach, California.

In the following chapters, members of the OTS teams in Connecticut, Pennsylvania,[11] and California share how they too came to be involved in OTS. After reading their stories, read the testimonials of a few of the formerly homeless who are no longer living on the streets because of OTS.

Will the next chapter begin in *your* community? To learn more about how you can form a chapter of OTS and help the homeless begin new lives in newfound homes, turn to page 93. When you are convinced that this is the next step you need to take to help the homeless where you are, contact us at

OFFTHESTREETSNOWSTARTUP@GMAIL.COM

We look forward to hearing from you!

---

[11] Members of the Lancaster team, from left to right: Al Gillis, John Pecorari, Chuck Mayo, George Stadler, Jack O'Donnell, Jean O'Donnell, Don Cronauer, Pat Maxwell, Sue Donnelly, Erica Gerhart, Nancy Bogda, Nancy O'Conor, Mary Peterson, Tom O'Conor, Roger Peterson, and Bill Allison.

"Though it is true that this mission demands great generosity on our part, it would be wrong to see it as a heroic individual undertaking, for it is first and foremost the Lord's work, surpassing anything which we can see and understand. . . . God takes the initiative. . . . 'he has loved us first' (1 John 4:19) and . . . he alone 'gives the growth' (1 Cor. 3:7)."

Pope Francis, *Evangelii Gaudium*, 12

Photo of Deacon Michael Oles, Danbury Goodwill Store Manager Al Thistleton, Joe Simons, and formerly homeless Louise.

OFF THE STREETS Team Members

JOE SIMONS, OTS DANBURY

My name is Joe Simons. I worked for IBM for 29 years, and for the last 25 of those years I volunteered at Dorothy Day Hospitality House, a soup kitchen and shelter in Danbury, Connecticut. My original motivation for working with the homeless was a kind of guilt—not the noblest of motives. In fact, it was many years before I realized that working with the homeless is what I was really called to do. Now that I'm retired, I still volunteer at Dorothy Day, and spend even more time there.

> One of the most amazing things about OFF THE STREETS is that although we give our time and talents to help the homeless, we receive so much in return, sometimes in unexpected ways.

I originally started at the Dorothy Day shelter because it fit in well with my schedule. The shelter is open only at night. The guests come at 9:00 PM and are out at 6:00 in the morning, and there is the opportunity to get a couple hours of sleep during that time. At Dorothy Day House we take real pride in the fact that we are an all-volunteer organization. The shelter sleeps sixteen people and the soup kitchen serves about 80 to 100 people a day. I don't think there are many other shelters and soup kitchens operating at that scale exclusively with volunteers. Most have some kind of staff. But we've always been all volunteer. It's a basic shelter: we provide a safe, warm place for people to stay, but we don't have social workers or other services on site. We're just a bunch of regular people who stay there at night and go back to our lives in the daytime. We've always been very careful to make sure we're doing what we're doing as well as we can, but there was always a line we wouldn't cross. We would always refer people to the existing social service infrastructure in Danbury if they were interested in permanent housing.

I met Deacon Mike Oles at Dorothy Day House about twenty-five years ago. We were both shelter coordinators and I got to know him quite well. In a variety of ways, he crossed over that line we had and got involved with some of the shelter guests and actually helped them to get into housing. It was after he'd been doing this informally for a while that he decided to start a formal organization, which became OFF THE STREETS.

We had big meetings, and there was a lot of enthusiasm. I'd go to the meetings and was officially the secretary. But Mike was doing all the day-to-day work and having the real contact with the people we were helping. After about a year and a half, I could see that the work was overwhelming for him. Phone calls and other inquiries were pouring in faster than he could respond to them and many calls went unanswered. I thought the idea of OFF THE STREETS was a good one, but we just needed a more organized way of doing it.

I was eligible to retire, so I talked to Mike and said, How would you like it if I came on board full-time to work with you, side by side, and get this thing running as efficiently as possible? He told me to talk to my wife and pray on it, which I did.

So, in May 2011, I retired from my job at IBM and started to work with Mike on OFF THE STREETS on more or less a full-time basis. We developed a standard approach to dealing with requests for help. For example, we set up our phone system through Google Voice, which was really helpful because we communicated a lot with people over the phone. Through Google Voice we were able to log all the calls in and all the calls out and get some control over the whole process, and that made a big, big difference, because it enabled us to return all the phone calls and get back to people on a timely basis. We used Google Docs to document individual cases and to keep track of people we were helping.

> The idea behind OFF THE STREETS is such a simple one. . . . we turned this idea into a reality.
> We found out what works and what does not work
> We built a good foundation.

We also worked on the furniture business. We had collected a lot of furniture and needed to understand what we really needed. We weeded our existing inventory and decided to accept only basic furniture, mainly for single people moving into a room or a studio apartment: twin beds, small tables, small chairs, etc. We stopped accepting couches, china cabinets, and just anything people wanted to donate. A volunteer stepped up to keep an inventory so we could know what we had in storage at any time. Although we didn't have a lot of storage space, what we did have was useful and accessible.

Because Mike and I were working side by side every day, we were able to help people very quickly. I'll never forget the first time we managed to get someone out of the shelter and into a fully furnished place of their own within forty-eight hours of the initial inquiry. One of our shelter guests called us and said he knew of an apartment that was available. We talked to the landlord and I was able to give her a check the same day, and the next day we delivered a whole small apartment full of furniture. When it was over, Mike and I marveled at how easy it had been to do it. Then we realized that an immense amount of thought and hard work had gone into getting things organized. But even more important, this was not our work but the Holy Spirit working through us.

One of the most amazing things about OFF THE STREETS is that although we give our time and talents to help the homeless, we receive so much in return, sometimes in un-expected ways. For example, one Thursday in early April I received a call about a family of four (a mother I'll call Inez and her three children) who needed help with a security deposit. Inez was a victim of domestic violence and was moving to Danbury after receiving a Section 8 voucher. She said she had heard about an available three-bedroom apartment that sounded attractive, but she needed to sign the lease and pay the security deposit right away. She sounded very anxious, so I agreed to meet her at 5:00 that afternoon.

Inez arrived at the apartment, which was half of a two-family house, with her three kids. The landlord met us at the door and showed us, with obvious pride, how he had fixed up and refurbished the place.

Inez and the kids were delighted with the apartment, and all the paperwork was signed on the spot. The relief on Inez's face was apparent. At this point I expected that all three parties (the landlord, the tenants, and I) would go our separate ways. However, the landlord invited Inez, her three kids, and me into his home in the other half of the house. He proudly introduced his family— wife, son, and daughter—and they made us feel welcome. The daughter took Inez's kids to the playroom and entertained them. The landlord proceeded to lay out a spread of food for us and would not let us leave until we had eaten our fill. Throughout the meal, Inez wept occasionally with joy and relief.

I was really touched by the landlord's generosity and hospitality. I've met a lot of landlords through OFF THE STREETS. Most of them seem like good people, but I've never experienced anything like this.

When I got home, I told my wife about what had happened and then looked at the calendar. It was Holy Thursday. It dawned on me

Now it's time for others who have received the calling to follow in our footsteps.

that, like the Apostles at the Last Supper, Inez's family and I had just had our feet washed (figuratively, of course).

The idea behind OFF THE STREETS is such a simple one: that homeless people with a source of income can rapidly escape homelessness and get into a place of their own. Through our experiences in Danbury, we turned this idea into a reality. We found out what works and what does not work. We built a good foundation, and now it's time for others who have received the calling to follow in our footsteps.

I have been a volunteer at our local food bank for many years, collecting and delivering food to families in need in our community. Many of these families and individuals have difficulty paying their rent and some are homeless. I had seen firsthand that there is a great need to help the homeless, especially veterans, in our area to obtain housing.

One December day, a group of volunteers had just completed our Christmas food deliveries when I received a phone call from Deacon Mike Oles. He was looking for volunteers to move a sleeper sofa off his front porch and deliver it to a woman in Danbury whom Mike had helped to get OFF THE STREETS and into a one-room apartment. She had no furniture and was sleeping on the floor. Several of us delivered the couch to her and she was thrilled. I told Mike to give me a call if he needed more help.

I believe it was through the work of the Holy Spirit, and Deacon Mike's determination, that we found a clean place to store the household goods needed by those we help to place in new homes.

Soon he called and asked if I knew of a place to store furniture and other household goods until they were needed. After several attempts that didn't work out, a good friend and fellow volunteer was able to procure storage units from a local businessman. I believe it was through the work of the Holy Spirit, and Deacon Mike's determination, that we found a clean place to store the household goods needed by those we help to place in new homes.

Deacon Mike invited me to a meeting of OFF THE STREETS and later asked me to be on the board of directors. My primary responsibility is collecting small furniture, appliances, and other household goods. We accept donations of these items on the first Saturday of each month at a local church in the center of town that also houses our food bank.

I feel blessed to be a small part of OFF THE STREETS. Thank you, Deacon Mike, for starting this ministry, and thank you, Joe Simons, for continuing this important work.

PAUL PALANZO, CERTIFIED INSURANCE COUNSELOR AND VICE PRESIDENT, ROSE & KIERNAN, DANBURY, CT

Over the years, my wife and I have volunteered at the Dorothy Day Hospitality House shelter in Danbury, Connecticut. During those times we have seen many of the same individuals seeking shelter from the elements. Some of these people are employed but cannot afford to make the leap from homelessness to having their own apartment. OFF THE STREETS is a Godsend to them. It restores dignity with a sense of accomplishment. God bless OFF THE STREETS for being there for them.

GEORGE STADLER, OTS LANCASTER

I attended the OFF THE STREETS informational meeting at St. John Neumann in March 2013. The next day I reviewed the OTS website with the director of the Lancaster Homeless Service Providers Network and asked him if he thought the mission of OTS was realistic. He thought it was a good idea because it would provide a missing piece rather than duplicating existing services. I prayed about what I should do next and attended the first organizational meeting, where I heard about the different jobs that needed to be filled. I prayed some more and told Deacon Mike that I wanted to help but not as the "main man." He told me another person had also stepped forward and suggested that we could be "co-administrators." So now I am sort of the main man every other month.

I like that OTS has a concise mission of providing a security deposit and furniture rather than trying to take on the entire spectrum of homelessness. I am inspired by God's grace reflected in the loving attitude of all the others who responded to help form the Lancaster chapter.

MATT WENTZEL, OTS LANCASTER

Although I do not get the opportunity to serve OTS in a big way as far as time commitment, I remain committed to the cause. The mission is something in which I involve my young boys (Luke, 10; Adam, 8) to let them know how others are in need and to help them understand the concept of humbleness. I still hear them recall me giving a homeless man a sandwich and a bottle of water on a Pittsburgh park bench some years ago. At first they were a bit afraid, but later, after discussion, they realized that, despite his rough appear-

I took care of homeless people while working as a city of Pittsburgh paramedic. . . . They were people with a story when the exterior was stripped away.

ance, the man had a story, and a mother and father just like they do, and that he is a person in need.

When I took care of homeless people while working as a city of Pittsburgh paramedic, I felt a sense of helplessness for them as I knew that I was putting on a proverbial Band-Aid when I took care of them—not really helping their long-term situation. They were people with a story when the exterior was stripped away. As a sociology professor once told me, "Do not judge until you walk a mile in their shoes."

What keeps me interested in this wonderful program is feeding off of the tireless energy of fellow parishioners, like the Thompsons. They have a zeal for helping and that feeds me to do more. This really is what my concept of Jesus is all about: helping fellow men truly in need without judgment. It fills me with sorrow and joy to take part in this mission.

Thank you for rolling this out in Lancaster, especially Manheim Township, where we all have so much.

Don Cronauer, OTS Lancaster

What made me get involved? I had been voluntarily sleeping with the homeless for years, so I have seen what it is like not to have a place to stay, and I have seen how hard it is to get out of that rut once you are in it. I also know how close some of them are to being able to have their own place. The majority of these unfortunate people try hard, but

> The majority of these unfortunate people try hard, but they just need a helping hand to get the ball rolling.

they just need a helping hand to get the ball rolling. It is also inspiring to see how they help each other—as best they can with such limited means.

What makes me stay? Because what we do is still needed. I am also very pleased with the group of people who are involved. Every person in our group has a function and is proud and glad to perform it.

BARBARA CARR, OTS LANCASTER

Last Christmas I was sorting gifts that were donated from the Giving Tree when I noticed a large pile of gifts for homeless children. For the first time, I realized just how many homeless children there are in our backyard. In my mind, we were in an area where there could not be any homeless children; we are not living in a third-world country. My heart broke. It is terrible enough for an adult to live on the street; again this is something I really can't fathom. I take for granted my nice home, good food, warm bed, nice clothes and many conveniences (too many conveniences). But to think that a child would not have these things, especially at Christmas, put a hole in my heart. It was at that moment I decided I had to help these children.

> I take for granted my nice home, good food, warm bed, nice clothes, and many conveniences. . . . to think that a child would not have these things . . . put a hole in my heart.

For the next few months I tried to think of some way to help them on my own, but everything I thought of would put more of a burden on our parishioners, who seem to be asked to buy or donate to something almost every week. I prayed for help and the Holy Spirit gave me the idea of the Loose Change Project, in which parishioners would be invited to drop coins into a large jug located in the lobby as a way of raising funds. I mentioned this idea to Tom and told him I was going to go to the Ladies Auxiliary and ask if they would sponsor the project. Tom told me he had just heard of the OFF THE STREETS program. I realized it would be the perfect fit. Considering the size of our parish, *if everyone would give just four cents every Sunday of the year, we would be able to take six families off the street.*[12]

In my mind, homeless people had no money and no source of income. But as I found out, that is not always the case.

Thank you so much for starting such a wonderful organization!

THOMAS CARR, OTS LANCASTER

I recall when I went to the first meeting of OTS Lancaster, one of the things on my mind was, if we get a homeless person into a rental by paying the upfront money, where will the monthly rent come from? In my mind, homeless people had no money and no source of income. But as I found out, that is not always the case. Many do have some means of income and, with the help of other homeless

---

[12] From its beginning in November 2013 through March 2014, the Loose Change Project has raised $2,770 for OTS. In the beginning, donations were larger; they now average about $80 per week.

organizations (that provide meals, clothing, and so on), they could pay the rent and have a home. One of the homeless people who came and spoke to us had a monthly income but, due to stealing at the shelters and his sharing with other needy folks, he never had the opportunity to save enough to get started. Hearing that really made it clear to me how and why OTS is needed and how it could be successful.

At the first meeting in Lancaster, Deacon Oles stressed that OTS was going to work with very little structure, very few rules and bylaws, and no paid employees. Coming from the business world, I thought that would be impossible. You convinced us that if we really wanted OTS to work, the Holy Spirit would guide us and it would happen. And it did! We learned that it is much, much more important to stay focused on the outcome than on paperwork or rules. OTS is intended to be loosely organized but focused on the results. We did not start out with a formal outline and structure. We thought logically about what would be needed, and it began to happen. Gerry said he had a trailer, then someone else talked about the possibility of storage, and it just rolled along, without structure but with focus.

We learned that it is much, much more important to stay focused on the outcome than on paperwork or rules.

Thank you, Deacon Oles, for your commitment and the generosity of your time.

For some time I'd been harboring the feeling that the Lord had been very good to me in so many ways, yet I'd done precious little to show my thanks. I try to follow my faith, I enjoy a wonderful family life, and I take comfort in a great circle of friends. I have all the material goods I require, am fulfilled by an assortment of hobbies, and generally live the good life without much consideration for those who are less fortunate.

Seeing people whose rough breaks, poor decisions, or other twists of fate had put them in such terrible straits lifted out of their abyss and given another chance was beyond uplifting.

When the meeting to discuss the OFF THE STREETS program was announced at church, I was curious enough to attend. When the true plight of the homeless was presented, I was definitely moved. It was particularly upsetting to learn how things really were less than ten miles from my comfortable residence.

When I heard how well-thought-out the OTS program was, about its experience in another region of the country, and that a chapter was starting in Lancaster, I decided to give it a try. I could always chicken out if it took "too much" sacrifice or cut into my selfish lifestyle more than I could handle, right?

I own a pickup truck, so I not surprisingly found myself on the furniture committee. After a couple of moves, I was totally hooked. Seeing people whose rough breaks, poor decisions, or other twists of fate had put them in such terrible straits lifted out of their abyss and given another chance was beyond uplifting.

Channeling donations of cash, used furniture, and other living needs into the lives of those who are so much less fortunate provides them with the opportunity to regain their self-respect and the fullness of life that I had taken for granted. Sometimes I get the feeling that the Lord is saying to me, "Now you finally get it, huh, Jer?"

ENRICA GERHARDT, OTS LANCASTER

Twenty seven years ago, a beautiful baby boy was born with a serious heart defect.

Within twenty-four hours, a team of doctors operated on the walnut-sized heart in an effort to save the child. Although the infant lived, eight months later more surgeries were necessary to keep him alive. A massive stroke during the third operation left the child blind, deaf, immobile, and unresponsive. The diffused brain injury overtook the surviving baby. He learned "to walk by faith and not by sight." Years of therapy began in an attempt to "reprogram" the boy's brain, with the help of many church volunteers. Meanwhile, family, friends, parishioners, nurses, and all others who were aware of his needs prayed, storming heaven for God's healing touch.

How valuable it is to work together to accomplish wonderful things.

Gradually, partial vision returned; eventually he could walk, run, bike, but not drive; he could hear better on one side than the other; his speech cleared up; he faced academic challenges but graduated from a two-year college; and his smile touched everyone's heart. As he grew older, he always looked at the things he *could* accomplish with

God's blessings, rather than at what he couldn't do. Taking care of the body that God had saved became part of his daily activities: eating healthy, exercising, growing strong, volunteering—and smiling.

One day he helped load heavy furniture onto a truck and unload it for a family using OTS. He was surprised when they told him how much they appreciated what he was doing and he shared how "rewarding it felt." As part of the "moving" team he learned how valuable it is to work together to accomplish wonderful things. Through OTS, he now has the opportunity to pass on his energy, love of life, and love of the Lord by helping others as so many others helped him many years ago! God saved him and has a plan for his life, which is now beginning to unfold as he learns to be one of God's servants. Thank you, Lord, and God bless everyone!

He now has the opportunity to pass on his energy, love of life, and love of the Lord by helping others.

KATHLEEN OLES, LANCASTER, PA

It can't be stressed enough, it seems to me: if you want to start a chapter of OFF THE STREETS, you first have to get some experience with the homeless. You have to spend time with them and get to know them a little.

While Mike was a volunteer and coordinator at the shelter in Connecticut, I visited a couple of times, but I never stayed overnight. I also never really got involved with the Dorothy Day soup kitchen, because during the day I either had kids with me or I was working. But because Mike was so involved with homeless people, sometimes they came knocking on the door of our house. They would come and ask Mike for money, and he gave it to them if they needed it, he was so generous. I wasn't always happy about that. Homeless people need things, and sometimes they need them so badly, I was afraid they'd come to our house when we weren't there and steal things. But after I got to know some of them, I didn't think that way anymore. I don't think that's the way most of them want to go.

> **A women's shelter in Lancaster needed a few people to stay overnight and Mike asked if I would go with him. I said sure . . . because it wasn't really Mike asking me, it was the Lord. And you don't say no to the Lord.**

Recently, a women's shelter in Lancaster needed a few people to stay overnight and Mike asked if I would go with him. I said sure, I'll go. I didn't really *want* to go. I just thought it would be *good* to go, because it wasn't really Mike asking me, it was the Lord. And you don't say no to the Lord.

The shelter and people looked like I thought they would, but it was a different kind of experience. The volunteers slept in two shifts. Mike and I took the first sleeping shift, from 10:00 to 2:00, when the others came in and woke us up. It was dark but we got up and put our stuff away so the other volunteers could use the room.

And those four hours of sleep were not really four hours, because it took me an hour to get to sleep. The sleeping arrangement wasn't comfortable. We were in an old exercise room and had only a mat to sleep on. I could not get down on the floor, so I put the mat on one of the exercise machines. It had a plank that was up off the floor a bit. I put my sleeping bag on top of that and just rolled in there. When it was time to get up it was easier. I would have had a hard time getting up off the floor.

So I did manage to sleep for a couple of hours. After I got up I got busy doing things, like setting up for breakfast. Then we had to start waking them up. The first person wanted to get up at quarter to four to go to work, and there were maybe six other people who wanted to be woken up at different times—4:00, 5:00. Everyone had to be up by 6:00. We made coffee for them and put out some Power Bars, but that's all

> They all thanked us very much for being there, for coming and staying. They shouldn't thank me. I should thank them, because they opened my eyes a little more.

they got. It looked like there were thirty or forty people there, and most of them knew what they were supposed to be doing. They brought their sheets out and put them in piles.

Some of the women were really tough. A lot of them did have jobs. One lady was dressed in one of those blue hospital uniforms. She was probably a nurse's aide. Why isn't she living somewhere? Why is she still homeless?

Another lady was there with her two daughters. She was older and her daughters were maybe in their thirties and twenties. The younger daughter was pregnant. The mother had a job and she was determined to get the daughter who was pregnant off the street. She was going to go talk to the agency that refers people to OFF THE STREETS. Mike told her, make sure you tell her you talked to me. It was her daughter's fourth time being pregnant. She'd had three other children. Two had been adopted by strangers, the third was adopted by her grandparents. She can't have any of them back until they're eighteen, and only if they want to come live with her. It's hard to have a child if you don't have a place to live, because that child will be taken away from you. There's something wrong with that whole system and the way these things are handled. Women especially shouldn't be living on the street.

I'm glad I don't need to stay there. I could. Anybody could. Anybody in the wrong circumstances could have to stay there. You never know where you're going to end up. Years ago I volunteered in a nursing home. It was just an average nursing home, in Texas. One lady there had been very poor and was on Medicaid. She was very nice and I would help her write letters. Right next to her was another lady. She had been a doctor or a lawyer or something. She sat in a big chair almost like a high chair and she could not communicate at all. They were both there, in the same place. So it doesn't always make any difference how you lived. Rich or poor, we are all going to end up in the same place. It just goes to show that money doesn't really buy you happiness. But it does get you a roof over your head—if you can find a place to live.

If you wish you could help these people more, think about starting a chapter where you live.

I would stay there overnight again. They all thanked us very much for being there, for coming and staying. They shouldn't thank me. I should thank them, because they opened my eyes a little more. The hardest part was the lack of sleep. We were really tired the next day, but they really appreciate it.

OFF THE STREETS is certainly helping a lot of people to get out of that, if they want to get out. If they want it and they have a job or get social security or something, OFF THE STREETS will help. If you wish you could help these people more, think about starting a chapter where you live.

DEACON KEVIN AND ELLEN MOORE, OTS BRIDGEPORT

Every year, in early November my wife and I attend the New England regional convocation of Roman Catholic deacons, where we meet with other deacons and get ideas on ministry. A few years back we attended a seminar on helping the homeless given by a fellow deacon from the Diocese of Bridgeport, Connecticut, Deacon Mike Oles.

> **As I pray the liturgy of the hours or listen to the readings at Mass, I am amazed at how often Scripture supports Jesus' counsel to help the less fortunate.**

I recognized him but had not formally met him before. We were very impressed by the work he was doing to help the homeless get a roof over their heads. The question in my mind as he spoke was, who is this man who came up with such a straightforward, effective means of helping people?

After the talk I went up to him and started asking questions, to my wife's embarrassment, about how he started this ministry. My wife thought I was questioning his credentials. What I was questioning was the qualifications needed to be so effective. I thought Deacon Mike must have been a social worker. To my surprise, I learned that he is a physicist and retired Air Force officer.

Remembering my mother's counsel to help those who are less fortunate, I could not let this ministry escape my mind, but both my wife and my spiritual director warned me that I did not have the time. A year or two later, in anticipation of retirement, this ministry moved to the front of my mind. Walking into the vesting room for a diocesan event, who is the first person I saw? Deacon Mike. To my surprise, he was visiting from his new location in Lancaster, Pennsylvania. The Holy Spirit works in amusing ways.

When I mentioned OFF THE STREETS to my spiritual director, he reminded me how over the years I had always expressed interest in helping others. My wife and I arranged a trip to Lancaster to get more specifics on the program from Deacon Mike and to attend a meeting of his new chapter. We now have our own chapter.[13] Volunteer response has

---

[13]Members of the OTS Bridgeport team, from left to right: Jane Baxter, Kevin Nicholas, Maureen Boda Ken Boda, Ann Pomponio, Fran Lichtenberg, Deacon Ray Chervenak, Jo Olsen, Ellen Moore, and Deacon Kevin Moore. Photo taken by Kevin P. Moore.

been wonderful. We are working on serving just one person at a time. Each day as I pray the liturgy of the hours or listen to the readings at Mass, I am amazed at how often Scripture supports Jesus' counsel to help the less fortunate. Please pray that the Holy Spirit will continue to inspire our chapter.

May the grace and peace of the Holy Spirit be with us all forever!

LARRY BURNS, OTS HUNTINGTON BEACH

My journey of learning how I might better serve the homeless community in Huntington Beach (HB), California, where I've lived for the past six years, began in the fall of 2012. My wife and I initially thought it would be a good idea to stock backpacks full of supplies, keep a few in our cars, and hand them out to the homeless persons we'd see while driving around. Before we started doing this, however, a Christian friend recommended that I spend some time with a local food bank or shelter to determine what the homeless really need.

In December 2012 I visited Beach Cities Interfaith Services (BCIS), a food bank that has served the homeless in HB for twenty-five years. There I met Bill Wright, a pastor and caseworker who has spent the past thirty years working with the homeless. Bill spent more than an hour giving me and my

> **A long-term homeless man . . . asked me to tell him how he could get OFF THE STREETS. I didn't have a clue. This question prompted me to begin my search for a way to help him.**

kids a tour of the BCIS operation. Then, for the next year, I worked with Bill as a BCIS volunteer.

I enjoyed getting to know the homeless people who came to BCIS and developed personal relationships with many of them, yet as I helped provide them with food week after week, I became saddened by two things. First, most of these people had no hope and no plan to get themselves OFF THE STREETS and out of their homelessness. Second, I wondered if giving them food week after week was actually enabling this sense of entrapment. I felt like we were putting a Band-Aid on a battle wound, and this depressed me.

OTS Huntington Beach has become a reality. . . . all of this has occurred without a single face-to-face meeting with anyone from OTS Central.

This all came to a head one evening in the fall of 2013 at an outreach dinner for the homeless. A long-term homeless man told me point blank that he wanted to get OFF THE STREETS but didn't know how and felt trapped. The clincher was when he asked *me* to tell him how he could get OFF THE STREETS. I didn't have a clue. This question prompted me to begin my search for a way to help him.

I started with a simple Google search on the phrase "how to get homeless OFF THE STREETS." The very first thing that came up in the search results was the website of OFF THE STREETS in Danbury, Connecticut. I was intrigued because they were very focused on getting the homeless into homes of their own by providing the upfront security deposit and initial household goods. The testimonial videos and the fact that they had placed more than two hundred people since 2009 was very compelling. I immediately

shared this information with Bill, and after a few discussions and prayer we both decided that I should contact OTS and ask if we could start an OTS chapter here in HB.[14]

I e-mailed OTS in October 2013 and then had an hour-long conversation with Joe Simons. After that phone call, Mike Oles contacted me and we agreed that we should pursue starting an OTS chapter in Huntington Beach. Several conference calls and e-mail discussions later, OTS-HB has become a reality. We are incorporated in the State of California, have selected our local board of directors, and have obtained our nonprofit 501(c)3 status under the group exemption umbrella provided by the founding OTS organization in Connecticut.

I would like to note that all of this has occurred without a single face-to-face meeting with anyone from OTS Central. Mike and I agree that we are following the promptings of the Holy Spirit through all of this. Each conference

---

[14] Members of OTS-HB stand in front of a picture of the city's old Main Street. From left to right: Pierre Charette, administrator; Dave Moses, spiritual advisor (director of community outreach, First Christian Church of Huntington Beach); Cheryl Lynch, treasurer; Larry Burns, president; Bill Wright, chairman.

call starts with a prayer and we are all seeking to obey Jesus' command to help "the least of these" through our work with OTS.

The OTS-HB team has completed our government paperwork and local leadership and volunteer assignments, and we have already done some fundraising. We are up and running, with the shared vision to help the homeless by replicating the OTS model. With the guidance provided by Mike and Joe, and with God's help through the Holy Spirit, we are well on our way.

BILL WRIGHT, OTS HUNTINGTON BEACH

I came into a personal relationship with Jesus in 1974. I began my journey by going into the streets of downtown Santa Ana, California, to share how much God loves the homeless and poor. I wanted to find out how many friends I could make who didn't have a roof over their heads.

They would come back for the same things day after day. My family and I continued to minister in the only way we knew how.

This was very exciting for me and I still have some of those friends from the early years. My family ministered to the homeless by buying them breakfast, lunch, or dinner. During the early years of ministry we opened our home to homeless individuals and families to live with us.

I also felt called to preach and be a pastor, so I went to a private Christian university and was ordained. I have pastored churches in California and Hawaii. All of them were involved in some sort of ministry to the homeless or in feeding the poor. We even filled a couple of lunch trucks with food and went into parks to feed the homeless where they lived.

Each time we ministered to the homeless—through food, gas, or clothing—a need was met, but they would come back for the same things day after day. My family and I continued to minister in the only way we knew how.

After I'd been many years in ministry and in the pulpit, the Lord decided to send me back to school to become a board-certified chaplain. I worked in hospitals throughout Orange County, California. My official title was director of pastoral care. While the Lord had me in these hospitals, many homeless neighbors and friends came in with a

Building relationships . . . is what it's all about.

variety of illnesses and wounds. I also served on institutional review boards, on bioethics committees, and on interdisciplinary teams for the ICU, CCU, and ER. It was in this capacity that I learned deep lessons in humility. Combined with the Lord's grace, mercy, and compassion, this experience helped me to become friends with patients and their families.

I finally settled into the ministry that God wanted for me when I began working as a case manager with Beach Cities Interfaith Services (BCIS), a full-service agency that was established to offer emergency services to low-income families and the homeless in Orange County. BCIS offers food, clothing, hygiene, transportation, prescriptions, utility bill payments, birth certificates, IDs, Internet access, and job referrals in addition to case management. Through BCIS I get to support my friends and neighbors who are poor and homeless, in the process building relationships with them, which is what it's all about.

When I train volunteers I tell them that the people we serve can't make choices for themselves, such as where to sleep, what water to drink or shower in, where to go to school, what to eat, and where to get medical care. These are the poor and homeless who are on God's heart.

Luke 4:4 says, "No one can live on food only." I work with a great servant in the person of Larry Burns. I trained him and we built a strong friendship. After a year at BCIS, he said to me, "They keep coming back—the same ones. Nothing has changed for them." It was then that I realized that food alone doesn't bring change. It's a temporary fix. We were busy putting a Band-Aid on a gaping wound.

Larry and I got together for lunch many times and tried to figure out what could bring real change: maybe a place for the homeless to lay their heads at night, a place to call home, a place where they would feel safe, a place where they could go to sleep with confidence and without the danger of being beaten up or having their belongings stolen; a place where, if they had a job, they could get up in the morning, take a shower, and go to work with the knowledge that they have a place to come back to that is their own. We prayed together and concluded that the homeless need to know they are loved and safe, and we needed to find a way to help them. That attitude began to shape our thinking and daily activities.

> **Food alone doesn't bring change. It's a temporary fix. We were busy putting a Band-Aid on a gaping wound.**

Then one day Larry said, "Bill, I want you to look at OFF THE STREETS, a homeless ministry in Connecticut." I did, and the rest is history. Instead of just watching, we got involved. We got permission to use the name and to be affiliated with the founding group. They helped us step by step and it was easy.

At BCIS, Larry and I are affiliated with other agencies who have resources to help homeless people get jobs, and when they do, OTS is able to help get them into housing. Once they have a job and housing, they have hope—*that* is change. Good news for the poor is to bring them out of their poverty; good news for the homeless is God's love and a roof over their heads.

True religion works from the inside out. What you believe is expressed by what you do. Find the weak and empower them, find the hungry and feed them, give the homeless choices, get them jobs and places to live. Choice is really a luxury that the homeless don't have when all they are trying to do is survive another day; they take what they can get. In providing homes for the homeless who have an income from working or from public assistance and just can't scrape together enough money for the required deposit and such, OTS fills a vital gap in ending their homelessness.

> **Once they have a job and housing, they have hope— that is change.**

The homeless situation is temporary for most, but moving on and getting situated again in housing requires us all to help. OTS is the perfect avenue. I encourage you, if you are considering starting your very own OTS: it's great—DO IT.

In 2013, during my 39th season as an income tax preparer, a friend who needed comforting called and I could spare only one hour. It made me stop and think, "Why am I doing this? I am so stressed and busy, but I'm not saving lives or souls." As soon as I got past the April 15th deadline, I knew it had to be my last. I was making money, but at what cost to relationships and to my health?

> A lot does go wrong for a lot of people, and the resulting evictions and foreclosures leave many people without a place to live.

I had read a couple dozen books about biblical principles of finance and felt that God was calling me to use the skills and assets He had entrusted to my stewardship to work for Him. I contacted my church, First Christian Church of Huntington Beach, to see what their new Community Resource Center was doing. They had me come in, I thought just to tell me about it, but they assumed I was signed up to start working—and I guess I was!

At the Resource Center, we meet people who need someone to listen to their situation, share Christ's love, give them spiritual and financial advice, lead them to available resources, and sometimes help out with bus passes, gas cards, and utility payments. Many of the people who come in are homeless, some are living on the street, some in cars, some are moving from friends' couches to shelters, and so on.

One day a fellow volunteer brought in a flyer about a two-day course on homelessness. I attended the seminar and learned about the chaotic life of trying to survive on the street, about how rapid rehousing was both cheaper for the community and a better way to start addressing the other problems of those who are experiencing homelessness, and I met other people in the community who also wanted to help.

I also became a certified online mentor for Crown Financial Ministries' MoneyLife service and began working with Christians who had gotten into financial crisis or who wanted to learn how to be obedient to God in this area of their lives. Almost all of the people I work with never had good instruction from their parents, school, or church on how God wants us to handle finances. How easy it is to succumb to our society's idea of getting

Rapid rehousing was both cheaper for the community and a better way to start addressing the other problems of those who are experiencing homelessness.

as much as you can, as quickly as you can, through easy credit and get-rich-quick schemes; and don't worry about tithing or saving—live for today. Nothing is going to go wrong—until it does.

A lot does go wrong for a lot of people, and the resulting evictions and foreclosures leave many people without a place to live. Add to that people who should have some transitional housing provision after leaving the military, prison, a mental institution, a substance abuse program, an abusive spouse or parents, and the result is a lot of people who are on their own and out on the street. As the book and Bible study *Invisible Neighbors* tells us, "if you don't see them, you're not looking."

Another book that had an influence on me was *Toxic Charity* by Robert Lupton. Good intentions are not enough.

We can sometimes do more harm rather than help when we do for the poor what they have the capacity to do for themselves. The poor can end up feeling judged and more dependent instead of learning skills to help themselves. Helping out in emergencies is one thing, but enabling a system to continue a cycle of handouts and dependence may make those who are providing the services feel better about themselves but does not necessarily help those who are receiving the services. If those being served are able to be partners in the process, they will feel more empowered. That said, it takes time to build relationships with people so that they trust enough to take advice and to want to get involved.

Everyone deserves another chance. Jesus did this for us, how can we not help others?

When I got a call about possibly being the financial person for the Huntington Beach OFF THE STREETS, I was very excited and researched the website of the already operating eastern chapters. This sounded like something that would be very positive, giving a hand up, not just an ongoing handout. Everyone deserves another chance. Jesus did this for us, how can we not help others?

OTS-HB is on its way! With help from Mike Oles and Joe Simons, we have put together our donor thank-you letters, opened a checking account, acquired the proper insurance, put together a brochure, and instituted financial controls and tracking tools. We pray that the Lord blesses and guides us and gives us discernment and wisdom to truly help, and that we utilize all the skills and talents He has bestowed upon us to serve Him and others.

The Formerly Homeless

MY NAME IS DANA. My life started Christmas Day 1983. I was born to alcoholic and drug-addicted parents. I grew up with my mom mostly, at times with my dad. I was given the most amazing little brother when I was three and a half years old. I had a horrible childhood. I was physically, mentally, and sexually abused. It was very rough growing up with these things happening to me and not being able to share the pains with anybody.

I was taken away from my mom at ten years old. I was put in four different placements. When I was sixteen I got emancipated. I had to fend for myself on the streets of the unknown. Sixteen is when my life was turned upside down, twisted and flipped all over.

I began homelessness at sixteen, sleeping in cars, under stairs, in twenty-four-hour laundromats, pregnant and all.

I was drugged and raped. One month later I found out I was pregnant. I didn't know what to do. At first I thought 100 percent adoption. Well, four months passed and the first movement my daughter made was when my decision changed. She was mine. My life changed for the best. I would keep her and do anything and everything for us. Key'Aja is my lifesaver. I began living from that day forward.

I gave birth June 25, 2001. I stayed with my mom until my daughter was almost one year old. My best decision in life was keeping Key'Aja.

I began homelessness at sixteen, sleeping in cars, under stairs, in twenty-four-hour laundromats, pregnant and all. I left my mom's when Key'Aja was almost one. I got my own place but because of domestic violence I lost it. I left with my helpless three-year-old daughter. I felt so bad, but I knew I had to do what I had to do to make sure we had a place to go so we went to a shelter. For about two years we were in and out of shelters, sleeping at friends' houses here and there. This was horrible.

Then I met the father of my other two children. I thought I was in love. Well, I thought wrong. I found out I was pregnant. The abuse started. I stayed because I thought I had nowhere else to go. Well, August 9, 2007, I gave birth to Zy'Airah and things seemed good. Four months later I got pregnant again. The abuse got even worse. I still stayed, hoping for the abuse to stop and to have a "happy family." Well, it didn't. I gave birth to my son Zay'Vion on October 6, 2008.

On November 14, 2008, I moved out and got my own place again. I got married to a good man on October 5, 2009. We are still married but separated. Things just didn't work out. Now, a mother of three children, I thought everything would get better. In reality, it's harder now with three children. I have been homeless two more times since then.

To everyone involved with the OFF THE STREETS program, the biggest and utmost respect, and thank-you to all who have given my family and me another chance.

THOMAS SENGEH, LANCASTER, PA

For a family that lives in abject poverty, education is never a priority. Survival has been and still is the watchword for us. This state has left me with fear not only of becoming a failure in life but also of becoming a burden to society. These fears have haunted me since childhood.

> Struggling for survival was the only option. ... My best friend was shot in my presence. The hardest reality is the sight of a friend struggling with blood on, and a bullet in, his head.

The dark days of my life started in 1996, when I was nine. I was abducted and taken to fight for a cause I can't explain. I was at school when the militia attacked my town in Sierra Leone. Struggling for survival was the only option for me and the other kids of my age who were abducted. Those who

---

could not meet our abductors' expectations were shot on the spot. My best friend was shot in my presence. The hardest reality is the sight of a friend struggling with blood on, and a bullet in, his head. Girls under the age of twelve were used as wives.

We were taken to Camp Zogoda, a training camp close to the borders of neighboring Guinea and Liberia, for what I now refer to as our "initiation" into the Revolutionary United Front movement. In this camp we were indoctrinated and introduced to the philosophy of the movement. "We are fighting for our rights. Sierra Leone belongs to all of us. We can't sit back and allow dictators and selfish individuals to overpower us. Do you understand?" We all shouted, "Yes, Sir!" That was the way we were required to answer the troop leaders and jungle commander.

My life was ruled by fear, insecurity, and lack of trust in almost everyone around me. That was our position in the jungle, where no one seeks refuge in the other.

Our commander for this training was a young man in his mid-twenties with a strange accent, similar to that of a Liberian. "My name is Commander Rambo," he told us. "Anyone who messes up will be killed. Our motto is 'brave, strong, and intelligent.' Therefore it is expected of you to be brave, strong, and intelligent fighters. Do you understand me?" "Yes, Sir!" a group of about five hundred boys shouted in a unified voice. The commander continued: "Our goal is to save Sierra Leone." This theme was buried in what we mostly referred to as the anthem of the movement.

My first mission was with a group of other fighters with strange faces. We were sent to recapture another training camp that had been captured by "peacekeepers." The mission, which lasted a week, claimed lives from both groups. In the end we were successful in capturing not only the base but ammunition too. We were already out of supplies needed for the missions ahead.

During six years of atrocities and brutal killing, my life was ruled by fear, insecurity, and lack of trust in almost everyone around me. That was our position in the jungle, where no one seeks refuge in the other. Food, a shower, and rest were never priorities in the midst of conquering our enemies (government fighters and peacekeepers). Life was nothing but a "cookie" in the eyes of an intoxicated "small soldier," as we were called. Toxic substances were injected into our bloodstreams to make us super high. Under the influence of these drugs, destruction was our ultimate goal. We "small boys units" and girls were also used as spies.

Food, a shower, and rest were never priorities in the midst of conquering our enemies.

Unfortunately for us, one time we were sent to spy on a battalion of Zambian peacekeepers at the northern headquarters town of Makeni. Our disguised appearance could signal to a trained battalion that our mission was not food. We were captured and encouraged to tell the truth about our mission in their camp. "We have no food, and we are town boys living in the neighborhood," we said. Our persistent claims and denials brought about rapid questions to which we could not find appropriate answers. We considered ways of maneuvering the situation, but our efforts proved fruitless. They opened a question-and-answer session: *Who are your parents? Where do you live? Are you willing to take us to your parents?* We said we would take them to our parents. A military truck of food and some peacekeepers escorted us. We pretended to forget our addresses, but they were very patient, knowing fully who we were.

We were taken to the headquarters for further questioning. We were encouraged to say the truth, but doing so would be considered a betrayal of the movement. Their diplomacy proved useless. Corporal punishment was the next option. After days of torture and starvation, we revealed the truth, which led to their recapturing other boys and girls from the rebels. We were handed over to Caritas, a Catholic charity, for family reunification. After almost a year in the camp, all the other kids were reunited with their biological and foster parents. I became the only one without information to trace my family. After a month or two, I was asked to move. I lived with a man who eventually became my stepfather. He found my mum, grandmother, and younger sister.

I met a man from . . . USA, who was doing voluntary work with child soldier/street boys like me. He encouraged me to be positive and to focus on my studies.

Adapting to normal society was one of the biggest challenges I had to face. After my long years in the jungle, I was not accustomed to normal ways. Fear, insecurity, and violence were the forces that ruled my life. I became an odd personality in the midst of others, inpatient with almost everyone, especially when provoked to anger. This was of course the way of life in the jungle. Living an unchosen life had been a punishment all by itself.

Despite my situation, I was very devoted to my school work. As a result, I emerged as the best student of my high school graduating class. Because of my outstanding performance, I was given a scholarship to the University of Sierra Leone, where I completed three semesters.

In 2008, I met a man from Lancaster, Pennsylvania, USA, who was doing voluntary work with child soldier/street boys like me. He encouraged me to be positive and to focus on my studies. He helped my younger sister and me to complete our high school education. In 2013, I miraculously won the green card lottery—an electronic drawing that gives people from developing countries the opportunity to live and experience a better life in America. The parents of my friend from Lancaster were so happy to have me in their house. A warm welcome dinner—a strange dish made of rice, which is my country's staple food—was already on the table when I arrived on August 28 after a long flight. I chewed the food with excitement not because of its taste but because I was now in America. My friend, who usually called me "Salone bobor" in our telephone conversations, changed my name that night to "America bobor." *Bobor* is a way of describing a small boy in my country. My friend must have picked it up during his time working with child soldiers/street boys.

Months of searching for a job yielded no positive result. Being at home all day with no one to talk to brought sadness into my life. I thought about how people who are jobless in my own country have friends to hang out with for the rest of the day without worrying about being fired from their jobs. I thought America would be the same, but in fact you will find company only on the screen, and I'm not a TV fan. I became bored and lonely.

Excitement came when I got my first interview, which was unsuccessful because of distance and my lack of knowledge of the American job market. Another friend and his wife encouraged me to attend a job fair, where I met my current employer. After a series of interviews, I was offered a job as a housekeeper, which pays a little more than the minimum wage.

My worries started again over securing an apartment and paying the debts which I had incurred prior to my coming. After meeting all of these commitments, I barely had anything left to meet my basic needs. In this state of mind, I met a friend who introduced me to an organization called Off the Streets. I wasted no time in calling the coordinator, who was so happy to help me with the security deposit once a place was found. To my surprise, they also provided me with furniture.

On a Saturday morning I had a call from Mr. and Mrs. Thompson that my room was ready. I was so excited, I ran to my new apartment. Upon my arrival, I met my room fully furnished with bed, lamp, dresser, towel, chair, table, and some cooking utensils. Filled with excitement, all I could say was thank you very much. Even now I will continue to say thank you to the Off the Streets mission and its benefactors.

"I am one of the ones that OFF THE STREETS has helped. I don't want you to think you shouldn't help yourself too. I stayed at the shelter to help myself out first, and then with their help I was able to move back into an apartment. So I really appreciate OFF THE STREETS for everything they've done for me."

Adapted from http://www.youtube.com/watch?v=Hma0Yxk9L3A&feature=youtu.be

"I give special thanks to OFF THE STREETS for helping me out

during a time of crisis. They set me up in my first apartment when I had absolutely nothing, and if it wasn't for them I would still have absolutely nothing, and I want to thank them very much from the bottom of my heart for pitching in and helping me out. Thank you very much."

Adapted from http://www.youtube.com/watch?v=iocdO6xJ-KM&feature=youtu.be

"My name is Daniel. I was homeless. I was living in Water-

bury in Tent City. A couple of childhood friends found me. They've given me a job, gotten me sober. I got a license, a bank account, a haircut, and an apartment. I'm very grateful. Through OFF THE STREETS I've gotten some bedding, a bed, an end table—things that you guys donated, and I am very grateful. I'm humble. I thank you so much."

Adapted from http://www.youtube.com/watch?v=eBQYjZUlsTg&feature=youtu.be

"I am a single father raising a son and the resources out here are not so great. An agency like OFF THE STREETS is something I needed and I greatly, greatly appreciate it. Everybody, thank you so much. Me and my son appreciate this and I just want to thank everybody."

Adapted from http://www.youtube.com/watch?v=HlAxPqSXAN0&feature=youtu.be

"My name is Jason. Thank you so much to the people that donated the furniture and the deposit money for me to get my own place finally. It was definitely a blessing from God and God bless everybody who had a hand in this. Thank you so much, I'm absolutely ecstatic. It will go to good use."

Adapted from http://www.youtube.com/watch?v=QZJmp8MYLuo&feature=youtu.be

"I'm Debbie. OFF THE STREETS and Deacon Mike and Joe have helped me tremendously. If it wasn't for them, me and my three children probably would be on the streets and I can't have that. I fought too hard for my children and they mean the world to me. So I appreciate it and thank you so much."

Adapted from http://www.youtube.com/watch?v=SLgLef6BiSE&feature=youtu.be

Recognition and Gratitude

FOLLOWING ARE SOME of the awards and letters of gratitude that OTS has received for its service to the community.

In October 2011, OFF THE STREETS was recognized with a Community Partnership Award from the Danbury Housing Partnership.

Also in October 2011, OTS was given the Community Partnership Award by the General Assembly of the State of Connecticut.

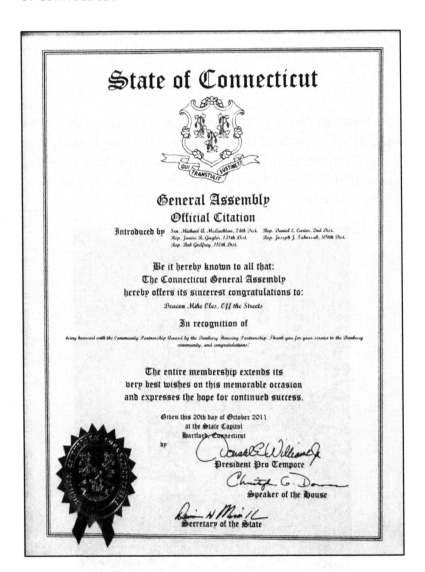

In 2014, OTS Lancaster received a letter of gratitude from the Supported Housing and Outreach Program of The Lodge Life Services, which helps persons with mental health issues to find housing.

THE LODGE
life services

Dear Friends,

The Supported Housing and Outreach Program (SHOP) works with homeless people who experience mental health issues. We work with landlords to locate permanent housing, which is not always an easy task. One of the obstacles we face as housing coordinators is lack of basic household needs like furniture and most importantly....security deposits.

Funding for rental assistance continues to dwindle and at times there are absolutely no funds available at the agencies we turn to for help. We have looked to Off the Streets to fill the gap. We can not express in words how much this organization means to the Lodge. When our clients are in need of a security deposit, furniture or other household goods, Off the Streets is there to help. Off the Streets has helped clients escape pending eviction which would result in re-entering the homeless system.

Off the Streets has been an extreme help to the people we serve.

This organization has been a God send to our clients and our agency. We can not thank you enough for the services, help and encouragement you provide to the community. From all of us at the Lodge, please accept our heart-felt thanks for all you do for our clients. Best wishes in 2014!

Warmest Regards,

Jessie Beiler
Francesca Castro
Iron Gonzalez
Program Coordinator

315 West James Street, Suite 106, Lancaster, PA 17603
Phone (717) 392-0257
Fax (717) 392-0102
www.lodgelifeservices.org

Transitional Living Center
Homeless Outreach and Veteran Services Programs
of Tabor Community Services
105 East King Street, Lancaster, PA 17602
www.tlclancaster.org

E-mail sent to Deacon Oles on June 13, 2014

On behalf of our team at Tabor and TLC, I would like to thank the OFF THE STREETS team for all of its assistance in providing security deposits for those who truly need it when leaving our program. Your exemplary model of giving is to be commended. Without your commitment and dedication to this effort we would not have moved as many households into permanent housing as we have in the past year. This not only provides a quicker exit into permanent housing for those leaving, but opens up a room for those truly in need on the streets or living in uninhabitable or often unimaginable situations. I commend you on your ease of process and the flexibility and speed at which this can happen.

Please understand fighting and ending homelessness is an ongoing battle. It is only with the collaboration and dedication of our friends and community partners that we can make strides toward that lofty goal. We thank you from the bottom of our hearts and pray that this teamwork continues on for as long as there are folks in need of permanent housing and experiencing homelessness.

God's peace to OFF THE STREETS and each and every one of you.

Doug Hopwood
Tabor Division Manager
(717) 397-3034   fax (717) 397-1782
dhopwood@tabornet.org

How to Start a Local Chapter of OFF THE STREETS

THE FIRST STEP in starting a chapter of OFF THE STREETS is to contact us at

OffTheStreetsNowStartup@gmail.com

The following outline is just an introduction to what else is involved. We are here to help you at any and every step of the way.

1. PUT A FACE ON THE HOMELESS

This step is *indispensable* to the success of any chapter of OFF THE STREETS. It's very difficult to empathize with the homeless without actually being directly involved with a homeless person once in a while. Volunteering at a soup kitchen or homeless shelter, with Habitat for Humanity, in a prison, for an AIDS organization, at a battered women's shelter, at a mental health facility or halfway house, in an emergency room, or in any other institution that provides services to the poor can help you to put a face on the homeless. Just striking up a conversation with a homeless person on the street can offer great insight. When we get beyond dealing with the homeless only intellectually, we become able to respond to homeless individuals as real persons in desperate need of homes of their own. Sometimes the homeless will be a husband and wife, sometimes a whole family, perhaps someone with young children who is living at a shelter for battered women. In any case, learning how they became homeless and what their daily existence is like is a humbling way of becoming fired up about helping them get OFF THE STREETS.

2. **Learn What OFF THE STREETS Does and How It Operates**

   A. Start by reading this book from cover to cover. Review especially the Frequently Asked Questions on pages 98–102, and the organization chart on page 95.

   B. Visit the OFF THE STREETS website at

   http://WWW.OFFTHESTREETSNOW.COM

   C. Contact OFF THE STREETS at

   OFF THE STREETSNOWSTARTUP@GMAIL.COM

3. **GET TO KNOW THE SERVICES ALREADY OFFERED TO THE HOMELESS IN YOUR COMMUNITY AND THE PEOPLE WHO OFFER THEM**

Most towns and cities already offer some degree of support to persons who have become homeless. Services may include emergency shelters, free meals, physical and mental health care, and other support such as help finding employment and housing. Learn how these existing organizations operate and how they work together. Connect with a caregiver or caseworker from an organization that operates or oversees one or more of these programs (such as Catholic Charities). Introduce yourself as a representative of OFF THE STREETS and talk to this "first responder" about the assistance that OTS would like to provide to the organization's clients.

OFF THE STREETS Structure

Central Organization		Chapters
• Provide advice and counsel • Provide tax exempt status to chapters • Conduct annual reviews	**Charter** ⇒ ⇐	• Follow OTS principles (all volunteers, minimal overhead, no government funding) • Obtain insurance • File required documents with IRS and state • Submit listing of expenditures and donations to central organization

Relationship defined in OTS Charter

4. HOLD AN OTS INFORMATIONAL MEETING

Arrange a place and time to hold an informational meeting about OFF THE STREETS and invite people to attend. This meeting should include the following elements:

A. Start with a prayer, asking for guidance from the Holy Spirit.

B. Pass around a sheet of paper for attendees to sign with their name, phone number, and e-mail address.

C. Introduce a homeless person who has been invited to share a little of what it's like to be on the streets.

D. Present what OTS is and how it operates.

E. Describe the OTS "jobs":

ADMINISTRATOR: oversees all activities within the chapter; acts as liaison with agencies whose clients meet the criteria for OTS help; runs monthly OTS meeting;

periodically reports, along with the chapter's treasurer, on the chapter's activities to the board of directors and OTS Central, providing information about persons being helped, donations, outlays, and other information that will need to be reported to the IRS and state government agencies; serves as final authority for implementation of fundraising and other ideas at the chapter level

SECRETARY: records and circulates meeting minutes; sends out reminders about the next meeting and its agenda

TREASURER: sets up a local bank account; makes and files copies of all checks received; deposits checks; writes checks; maintains a spreadsheet of deposits and withdrawals; sends thank-you notes to donors

FURNITURE COORDINATOR AND TEAM: take charge of furniture collection and outlays

LIVING NEEDS COORDINATOR AND TEAM: assemble and disseminate the "living needs" (kitchen, bathroom, bedroom, and other supplies) for each individual being moved into a room or apartment

IT COORDINATOR: sets up Google accounts (e-mail, voice, and document) and shows OTS team members how to access them; sets up and maintains chapter's website

FUNDRAISING COORDINATOR: pursues possible sources of funding

SPIRITUAL ADVISOR: a trusted member of the community, perhaps a clergy member; need not attend OTS meetings but provides support and advice as needed

F. Include time for questions and discussion.

G. Set a date and time for the first organizational meeting.

H. Offer a closing prayer.

5. HOLD THE FIRST ORGANIZATIONAL MEETING

A. Start the meeting with a prayer, asking the Holy Spirit for guidance.

B. Pass around an attendance sheet for everyone to sign.

C. The goal of the meeting should be to discover who is willing to volunteer for each of the jobs described at the informational meeting and to clarify what each person's responsibilities will be in the weeks between this meeting and the next. Between the informational and first organizational meetings, individuals may have contacted the person who organized the meetings to ask questions, volunteer for a particular role, or offer suggestions. These conversations and their outcomes may be shared at this meeting.

D. Set a date and time for the next meeting.

E. Close the meeting with a prayer.

Frequently Asked Questions

THIS CHAPTER ADDRESSES some of the questions that may arise as you think about starting a chapter of OFF THE STREETS in your community. If you don't find your question answered here, visit our website or contact us by e-mail.

What steps do we have to take legally to become a chapter of OTS? First, you must register as a corporation in the state in which you will be operating. This process varies from state to state and generally includes the following steps:

- Select a name and register it with the state.
- File Articles of Incorporation with the state.
- Obtain an employer identification number (EIN) from the IRS.
- Adopt bylaws.

As a nonprofit, you may be required by your state to file additional documents.

Each chapter must also agree to run its activities by OTS standards by signing the Charter for OFF THE STREETS Chapters, which outlines how OTS chapters operate and their relationship with the central organization. In return for complying with these requirements, you will receive IRS tax exemption under the OTS group exemption, which means that donations made to your chapter by individual donors will be tax deductible.

Prior to signing the charter, you must testify that you have done the following:

- Held an organizational meeting.
- Elected officers (administrator, secretary, treasurer, and so on).
- Adopted bylaws.
- Filed organizing documents to set up a corporation in the state you are in. The organizing documents must contain IRS language. We will help you with that.

Your chapter must agree to abide by the following OTS principles:

- OTS is a completely volunteer-based organization. There will be no paid staff.
- So that all funds will be directed to people in need, overhead must be kept to an absolute minimum.
- OTS receives funds through the generosity of individuals, churches, private foundations, and corporations. No money will be received from government sources. No one will be paid to raise funds for OTS.
- Members will not engage in any political activities or lobbying.

The chapter must also agree to do the following:

- Provide liability insurance as well as directors and officers insurance in order to protect volunteers.
- File all required state and IRS documents.
- Submit a recap of expenses and donations to OTS Central annually before January 31.

Each chapter will be reviewed annually by OTS Central. If it is determined that the chapter is not living up to the provisions of the charter, it will no longer be eligible for tax exempt status under the OTS group exemption.

How does a local chapter file taxes? Each chapter must file its own federal tax forms using the group exemption number provided by OTS Central after the local chapter is incorporated in its state and has obtained its federal EIN.

What insurance is suggested? Each chapter should obtain overall liability, director and officer liability, and medical coverage for volunteers. A chapter can obtain its own policy or use the same provider that OTS Central uses.

What reporting is required? Periodically, each chapter will report to OTS Central the number of people helped OFF THE STREETS. OTS Central can provide a simple tracking spreadsheet for this purpose.

What marketing is recommended? Chapters should obtain business cards and a brochure to hand out. OTS Central can provide a brochure prepared in Microsoft Word that local chapters can adapt to their own needs. OTS Central will create a tab for each chapter on the main OTS website (offthestreetsnow.com). We will provide a subdomain for each chapter, but someone from the local team will have to create and monitor the chapter's web pages.

What financial tools and controls are required? Each chapter should establish its own local bank account and use the financial tools of its choice (such as QuickBooks or an Excel spreadsheet). OTS Central can provide sample thank-you letters for donors. Receipts should be given for noncash donations.

How do we find the homeless people we can help and how do we determine who is ready and able to take responsibility for renting a room or apartment? There are two ways to identify those whom OTS can help: You can get to know homeless persons and their needs by volunteering at a soup kitchen or homeless shelter. You can also take referrals from local social service agencies. The first way of operating is how OTS got started, but over time we have learned the value of collaborating with the other local agencies that provide services to the homeless, and we now recommend relying primarily on referrals from these organizations, which are staffed by highly trained and educated individuals and teams who work daily with the homeless to determine their needs and resources. It is therefore important for new chapters of OTS to gain and maintain the confidence of those who work for these agencies. OTS team members must see themselves not only as servants of the homeless, but also as servants to the service providers who are in the trenches with the homeless day in and day out. Only then do we have the best chance of fulfilling our mission.

How should chapters communicate with the homeless and other agencies? OTS Central uses Google Voice to communicate with the homeless so that they don't have access to anyone's personal phone. Google Voice also tracks and documents every phone call with an e-mail transcript and audio recording. Agencies usually have direct access to OTS officers, with the understanding that this contact information is not to be shared with the homeless.

How may chapters raise funds? Local chapters may obtain funds by soliciting individual donors, churches, and other community or charitable organizations, any of which may organize fundraising events and activities. Also, grants can be requested from local institutions. OTS Central can provide examples of such grants that it has received.

What kinds of furniture and household items should we collect and how do we solicit, collect, and store these and other household items that people will need for their new homes? Chapters will need to get out the word about what items are needed, establish a drop-off time and location for donations, obtain a storage location, and arrange for volunteers and a truck to transport the items into storage and into the homes of the people OTS serves.

How is housing located? Generally the agencies that refer the homeless to OTS or the homeless persons themselves will find a potential housing opportunity. A list of potential landlords and properties can also be compiled by the local OTS chapter.

What are the demographics of the people whom OTS has helped to obtain homes? There have been more women than men, and about 20 to 30 percent of the newly housed have been children.

Should we follow up in some way with the people we have helped to get OFF THE STREETS? How do we monitor success? OTS has no formal system or process for following up on those whom we have helped to move into a room or apartment. If the person was referred by a social service agency, that agency will maintain contact and provide additional support as needed. If you want to follow up on a particular person, you can contact the agency to get an update or call them directly from the Google Voice number.

Compassion Always Trumps the Written Word

THE GUIDELINES PRESENTED in the preceding pages have been developed through trial and error and have proved to be the most effective means of fulfilling the core mission of OFF THE STREETS.

> Jesus said to them,
> "I ask you, is it lawful
> to do good on the
> Sabbath rather
> than to do evil,
> to save life rather
> than to destroy it?"
>
> Luke 6:9

There have been instances, however—and there may be for you as well—when the needs of a particular individual couldn't be met except by a leap of faith beyond the rules.

In the latter half of 2010, for example, OTS Danbury entered into an arrangement with Catholic Charities, ARC (Association of Religious Communities), and the regional government's mental health services department to house a man I'll call Brennan. A long-term veteran of homelessness, Brennan had great difficulty managing his anger, his grooming and attire, his money, and his alcohol consumption. He was barely able to function at the emergency shelters. All of these organizations considered him high risk, and if you looked at just the bare facts, it would seem clear that he couldn't make it. Still, we had agreed to pool our resources to help Brennan pay for an apartment.

Not everyone on the OTS team agreed with this decision, however.

There was no discussion of what I had done. It was as though, to them, there was nothing to discuss.

In the first year of OTS, while we were struggling to focus our mission and determine how best to carry it out, we had generated a lot of forms, organized in an impressive three-ring binder, intended to formalize our procedures. Determining who was eligible for our help and who was not required numerous discussions, and we had begun to function like a bureaucracy rather than looking at the person in front of us as the face of the Suffering Christ.

While I was far out of town dealing with a family matter, one team member, on the basis of our clearly written criteria, pulled OTS out of this collaborative arrangement, which caused it to collapse completely, because it would work only if every organization was on board. The landlord too, seeing this discord, decided to back out. When I returned, I spent several weeks attempting to rebuild the bridges that had been burned.

In the midst of this crisis I had dinner with several local priests. I was feeling as low as I possibly could. At one point during the meal I spent ten or fifteen minutes telling them what had happened. They listened. When I finished, one of them, Fr. Corey Piccinino, pastor of St. Mary Parish in Bethel, Connecticut, turned to me and said, "Compassion always trumps the written word." Then the three of them shifted the conversation to another topic altogether. There was no discussion of what I had done. It was as though, to them, there was nothing to discuss.

Despite the resistance and delay, my persistence finally bore fruit: the arrangement was reinstated and Brennan was placed in an apartment. We watched him like a hawk and provided lots of mentoring support. He remains housed more than three and a half years later.

And the three-ring binder? History. OTS abhors bureaucracy within its own operations. We learned our lesson: when in doubt, compassion does indeed trump the written word.

I never in a million years would have thought that Bill could provide any substantial contribution to getting people OFF THE STREETS. Yet . . . it was Bill . . . who performed this miracle.

Another story that illustrates the same principle began in 2009, soon after OFF THE STREETS started in Danbury. A man named Bill Shannon came up to me after Mass one day and asked to help with OFF THE STREETS. I thanked him but brushed him off, thinking, what could a man more than seventy years old do?

A few weeks later, he came up to me again after Mass and said, "Mike, I really want to help. Call me." I still couldn't think of anything he could do. He tried a third time, and I finally realized he was serious. To get him off my back, I told him about a man I'll call Sam. In my mind, Sam was a truly hopeless case. I could see no way that he could be helped. By sending Bill to him, I thought I was simply getting both of them off my back.

I had known Sam for many years. He had worked in Danbury, but when he lost his job, he had nothing—no benefits, no unemployment, nothing. He wanted to get another job, but then he had a stroke and became partially paralyzed. That stroke was followed by a second, which brought him close to losing his entire ability to walk and talk.

Sam's landlord was a kindly woman, but after three months of receiving no rent money from Sam, she was forced to evict him. I went to bat for him and the landlord in court, and she and the judge agreed to let Sam stay in the apartment for a few more weeks.

It was then that I referred Bill Shannon to Sam. Bill took the situation personally, as if Sam were his own brother. He met with Sam for breakfast several times, and took him to apply for Social Security disability benefits. It would be at least several months before Sam could begin to collect. Bill kept me posted about all he was doing, but I still could not see any possibility for Sam not to end up on the streets of Danbury during the brutal winter months. His life would become just another tragic homeless situation.

One day just before Sam was to be evicted, Bill announced that he had found a place for Sam to stay—a rehabilitation facility—and somehow Sam would not have to have any money to stay there! I still have no idea how Bill made that happen. Meanwhile, Bill stayed close to Sam, sharing meals with him and ensuring that he had everything he needed.

After six months, Sam's social security kicked in and Bill helped him find a place closer to Danbury so he could be near his friends.

Thinking as man does, I never in a million years would have thought that Bill could provide any substantial contribution to getting people OFF THE STREETS. Yet in one of the most intractable situations I have ever seen, it was Bill, empowered by the Holy Spirit, who performed this miracle—because the Holy Spirit is not bound by human reasoning.

Author's Afterword

OFF THE STREETS BEGAN with faith in God, and it continues with faith in God. OTS works because the members of the OTS team accept the guidance and gifts of the Holy Spirit:

> Courage
> Right judgment
> Wisdom
> Wonder and awe
> Understanding
> Knowledge
> Reverence

The actions resulting from these gifts are signs of the presence and power of God acting in and through the lives of the members of an OTS team. Every person with whom we interact—fellow members of the team, other caregivers, homeless persons, our benefactors, and all those with whom we come in contact—should see us as simply implementing the gifts we have been given by God for His greater glory. Rather than be praised for our actions, we would

Rather than be praised for our actions, we would rather be thankful that God has allowed us to be instruments of His Will.

rather be thankful that God has allowed us to be instruments of His Will. It is with this understanding that we undertake the awesome challenge of trying to assist those in greatest need—the homeless—armed with little more than our unshakeable faith in God. Every time we meet as members of the OTS team, we should remind ourselves, through prayer, of the utmost respect we have for the dignity of every human life.

If you are unable to start your own chapter but would still like to support the mission of OTS, please send a check made payable to OFF THE STREETS to the following address, and please tell us that you learned about our mission from this book:

OFF THE STREETS
PO Box 591
Bethel CT 06801

It typically takes about $500 to move one person or family OFF THE STREETS. All donations are tax deductible.

God bless you!

Publisher's Afterword

"The difference between 0 percent hope and 0.00001 percent hope is enormous." *Dan Beutler*[15]

EARLY IN 2008, I applied for a part-time job with a local retirement community. The application process included a thorough background check. Toward this end I was required to list all of the addresses I had called home during my entire life. When I was finished, I learned that my total number of official residences in less than fifty years was twenty-eight, if you count the three weeks I lived in a Tenderloin hotel after arriving in San Francisco in 1988, and the month in my early twenties when I lived in a rented fixer-upper until a week of rain revealed ceiling leaks in all the rooms. Fifteen of those dwellings were home for periods ranging from six months to a year and a half, and I managed to stay in three locations for nine years each (from ages 0–9, 9–18, and 35–44). For more than twenty of my adult years I have shared the costs of maintaining a residence with at least one other person, and for more than fifteen years I have lived alone and

---

[15] Dan Beutler is the husband of Congresswoman Jaime Herrera Beutler (R-Wash). Quoted in "Congresswoman's Miracle Baby Doing Well Nine Months After Doctors Said She'd Die," http://www.lifenews.com/2014/05/15/congress womans-miracle-baby-doing-well-nine-months-after-doctors-said-shed-die

been solely responsible for all expenses—including a year and a half when, though we were still married, my husband lived first with a succession of friends, then in shelters and hotels and sometimes in parks, and then in a yearlong substance abuse rehab program, while I paid all the expenses for our little cottage in one of the most expensive cities in the country.

During the first six months of that period, David was essentially homeless. I had told him that as long as he continued to use alcohol and drugs, he could not live with me. Was that the right thing to do? I don't know. Once during that period, after a three-day binge in a San Francisco hotel, he almost died—and would have if a willing stranger had not summoned medical personnel from a nearby emergency room, who arrived to find David not breathing and blue-skinned. They cut off his three layers of favorite shirts so they could get his heart beating again (I still have a large Teddy bear I sewed from the remains of those shirts), and they put a tube down his windpipe to restart his breathing. If he had died that day, I don't know how I would have lived with the regret I know I would have felt.

Soon after that incident he found his way into a yearlong program, and for almost a year after he graduated from it, he remained, as far as I could tell, sober. But then, for whatever reason, the downward spiral started all over again. He managed to get himself into another recovery program in California, and I, by that time needing a form of recovery myself, returned, with the help of his family, to the East Coast. Again, was that the right thing to do? I don't know, but at times I still wonder, what if?

David followed me to the East Coast not quite a year later. By that time I was renting rooms in the house of another woman and not prepared to live with him yet. He moved into his parents' house, the house he'd grown up in, and spent the next eight months or so helping them get ready to move into an apartment in a retirement community. He also got a job with a former employer—at a liquor store.

By Christmas Eve that year he was back in the hospital, detoxing. I stopped to visit him on Christmas morning on my way to his parents' house. On the basis of our conversation, I believed he no longer wanted to be married. In the next week I talked to a lawyer, and when I visited him on New Year's

Eve, I told him I would be filing for divorce. He looked as though a huge, heavy weight had literally been lifted off his shoulders—or so it seemed to me. Again, did I do the right thing? Again, I don't know, but I wonder, what if?

A few months later his parents had been moved into their new home and David was again, in a sense, homeless; that is, he was living in his brother's basement. And drinking. They told him the situation couldn't continue. He found a recovery program a couple of hours away that would take him. His brother delivered him there on David's forty-sixth birthday.

The formal program lasted thirty days. He then moved into a supervised residence, where he lived for six months while hunting for a job. After he landed one, he moved into an unsupervised house with ten or so other men in recovery. He stayed for three and a half years. Finally he moved into an apartment of his own—for the first time in his life. For him, it was a dream come true. Yet not quite a year later he was gone, dead from a drug-induced heart attack. He died alone (except for his two cats) and was found by a neighbor at least a day and a half later.

The fact that he did not succeed in remaining sober and alive is unrelated to the value of his life. His untimely death also does not invalidate the opportunities and support provided to him . . .

At the memorial service held on the grounds of the recovery program about six weeks after his death, several dozen people paid tribute to David. Virtually every one of them said, "He was my best friend." He was certainly mine. Despite all we'd been through that last decade, he was still the person who knew me best. Yet I remember a phone conversation during those last five years when he told me, "I'm everyone else's best friend, but who's mine?" Was I? I don't know. I do remember another phone conversation during the same period in which he told me, "You're the first person I call when I want to tell someone something good that has happened, because I can tell you're sincerely as happy about it as I am."

If I were allowed one do-over, it would be to say yes when a couple of months after he settled into his apartment he invited me to come stay with him for a week. "I've got wireless Internet. I'll give you a key. You can work while I'm at work. You can make it a retreat." I knew that if I went, it would break my heart to come back to my own apartment. I didn't want to go through that again. I'd given up. I wish I hadn't.

In the nine bonus years that followed that time when he would have died but didn't, the staff members and other residents of three rehab programs took a chance (and another and another) on David, as did several employers, landlords, and dozens of friends, coworkers, neighbors, and family members. The fact that, in the end, he did not succeed in remaining sober and alive is unrelated to the value of his life (to him and to all who knew and encountered him) during those nine years. His untimely death also does not invalidate the opportunities and support provided to him during those years—opportunities and support that should continue to be provided to others who have even a .00001 percent chance of success—the kind of support that OFF THE STREETS is willing to give to anyone who wants it.

> . . . opportunities and support that should continue to be provided to others who have even a .00001 percent chance of success.

Alice S. Morrow Rowan, Publisher
Not Forgotten Publishing Services

About the Author
By the Author's Wife

I MET MIKE IN SEPTEMBER 1963, during a mixer, one of those dances they used to have, at his college, Fairfield University, a Jesuit school in Fairfield, Connecticut. I was a student at Good Counsel College in White Plains, New York. We began visiting back and forth. He didn't have a car, so he sometimes came down on the bus and sometimes got a ride with another student going to meet his girlfriend. Sometimes I drove up to visit him in a car that was available to me. So I did all the driving when we were together, and it wasn't until four or five months after we met that I learned Mike wore glasses, with lenses as thick as coke bottles. Without them, he couldn't see anything at a distance, including me. I didn't care. I thought he was cute!

> Mike wore glasses, with lenses as thick as coke bottles. . . . He would start fires with them, in leaves and stuff, with the sun. He was always a scientist. He just wanted to see if he could do it.

Many years later he got Lasik surgery and didn't need to wear glasses at all for a long time. Now he needs them again. The ones he wears now are nothing compared to the ones he wore before. He could fry ants with them, and he did, when he was a kid. He would start fires with them, in leaves and stuff, with the sun. He was always a scientist. He just wanted to see if he could do it.

When I met Mike he was very quiet, very shy. He was totally a scientist-nerd kind of person. But he was so nice. I knew he was going to be the right one to marry. I don't know how I knew. I guess we just fell in love.

After college, Mike went into the Air Force. It changed him, in a good way. I think if he'd gotten a regular job in the science field, he wouldn't be the Mike he is today. He went to Officer Training School. In the Air Force they give you a lot of responsibility, put you in charge of something, right away, especially if you are an officer. Being in charge gave him a lot of confidence. He worked on the space program in Houston, then for DARPA, the Defense Advanced Research Projects Agency, in Florida. Working in these jobs he really, I think, figured out that he was smart—which I always knew (though Mike says it was both intimidating and a blessing to work in the midst of so many brilliant minds). In the Air Force he was forced to work with people, and he was so good at what he did that people listened to him as they worked with him. He became more and more outgoing and got really good at dealing with people. He rose through the ranks and became a lieutenant colonel and was put in charge of some big projects. He became like his father.

You think Mike is outgoing? You should have met his father. He was in politics—he was a First Selectman in his town. But he also worked for the factory, developing all kinds of needles. He helped to develop needles for heart surgery, and a needle for making pantyhose. But because he was just a factory worker, he never got any real credit for it. He was a very smart man, but he just went to grammar school, not to high school, and he put all of his sisters through school.

Mike was the oldest of six boys. His brothers were a little more boisterous than him, so he'd be the boss if he was around. They had a wild time. His mother would go into her room and pray just to get some peace and quiet, I think. She used to say, "I'm having holy hour."

So I think it was just a matter of time for Mike to bloom. And he did. People knew they could rely on him, that he would tell the truth, and that he would be there.

He left the Air Force in 1984. We moved back to Connecticut and he went to work in the civilian defense industry. He did that until he was laid off in 1998. I don't think he ever really liked it as much as the Air Force, but he stuck with it as long as he did because we had kids in college. I had just been made full-time at my job, so that was good. But we sold our house right away and moved into a smaller house.

> **After college, Mike went into the Air Force. It changed him, in a good way. . . . Being in charge gave him a lot of confidence.**

Maybe a year or two after we got back to Connecticut, somebody asked Mike if he wanted to help out in the homeless shelter one night a month. He said OK, he'd do that. He still had to go to work in the morning, so it was hard, but he did it. Eventually the guys that were running the place needed another coordinator, which is someone who opens the place every night for one week of each month. Another volunteer would come to stay with the guest, and then he would come home. He would leave to go there at around 8:15 or so and then be back home at 9:30 or 10:00. But sometimes, almost every month, he'd have to stay overnight one night because a volunteer wouldn't show up or would cancel. He became one of their top people.

We were both raised Catholic and we always went to church on Sunday, and we made the kids go to church. At one point we started going to daily Mass. I don't know how it happened. Mike didn't go as much as I did at that time, because he was working. One of the best things we did was go to a Marriage Encounter. That was a really good thing. We realized that our religion was really helping us with our whole life, that being Catholic and going to church was really a good thing for us. We were Eucharistic ministers for a long time. And we belonged to groups that would meet and talk about Catholic issues. When we came to Connecticut, we got very involved in the church—with the liturgy and in the choir, for a while, and doing other things. We have always been building on our faith, and talking together about it. We feel it is our faith that has helped our marriage and kept us together as a family. I think church and the spiritual life is needed by everybody—a spiritual life with a church base. You could say you have a spiritual life and not a church base, but it seems like it would be very hard to do it that way. If you belong to a church and contribute to it, if you are part of the bigger family of the church, you've got so much support from them. You need that. That's what brings you forward.

It was in 1996 or 1997, when he was still working in the defense industry and not liking that job, that Mike started thinking about becoming a deacon, after one of the priests in our parish approached him and asked if he'd ever considered it. And he decided to do it, because of the homeless. He was trying to help them but he didn't have any credentials, and he felt that if he was a deacon in the Catholic Church, it would give him more authority to help, to help from a church base.

That decision got tested right in the beginning. We had to go to Bridgeport and take a psychological test with something like 150 questions. It took about two hours. We took it with maybe twenty other couples. A few days later we got a call, or maybe it was a letter: something had happened to all the exams. They were thrown out by mistake and we all had to retake the test. I don't know, Mike said, maybe we ought to forget about this. You probably don't want to take that test over. I said no, we'll take it over again! We passed, and Mike was ordained in 2002.

> **We have always been building on our faith, and talking together about it. We feel it is our faith that has helped our marriage and kept us together as a family.**

Then he really got involved, in the parish and with the homeless. For a while we had only one priest, and Mike would help with every Mass, before, during, and after. Eventually we got another deacon, and then another priest, Fr. Corey Piccinino. He's the one who eventually told Mike, you've got to get this book done!

I don't know what he's going to do after this book. He used to play the piano a lot and very well. He says he can't just sit down and play again without lessons, so I want him to do that. He also wants to do more woodworking. But what he *really* wants to do, I think, is just start more chapters of OFF THE STREETS. I think it could start in a lot of other places very easily. So I think that's what he'll work on.

Kathleen Oles

Acknowledgments

IT IS IMPOSSIBLE for me to acknowledge everyone who had a part in the preparation of this book. Indeed hundreds, perhaps thousands of individuals, churches, and other institutions have shaped my thinking. Every good deed, every thoughtful essay and book contributed something. Many people showed me, more by example than with words, what it means to be a follower of Christ.

I am particularly indebted to everyone involved with the Dorothy Day Hospitality House in Danbury, Connecticut; to the parishioners at St. Mary Church in Bethel, Connecticut; and to their pastor, Fr. Corey Piccinino, who made me promise to write this book. The faith and enthusiasm of the teams in Lancaster, Pennsylvania; Bridgeport, Connecticut; and Huntington Beach, California who have started their own OFF THE STREETS chapters have inspired me to persevere in the effort to get the word out about what OFF THE STREETS is accomplishing and can accomplish.

Even with all this inspiration, however, there is one person without whom this book would not now be a reality. Lord knows I tried to write it on my own. Some of my earliest attempts are more than three years old. I tried everything, from buying "how to write" books and audio-to-text converters to just sitting at the computer and typing for hours on end. What I ended up with was three plastic bins full of documents and references, hours and hours of audio files, and a boatload of Word files. I was drowning in my own drivel, clueless as to how to proceed. I even Googled "ghostwriters" and "writers," but drew no closer to the goal. Then one day about a year ago I heard about Alice Morrow Rowan of Not Forgotten Publications.

At our first meeting, Alice learned a little about me and I learned a little about her. I quickly realized that she had more than just an intellectual understanding of what the book was to be about. Her strong faith in God and in His love and compassion for the poor has powerfully shaped, and been shaped by, many experiences in her own life.

My instructions to Alice were that the book had to be easy to read, with no wasted words, lots of visuals, and lots of motivational quotes. It had to motivate people who are already working in emergency shelters and soup kitchens, but are frustrated by the seeming inability of their guests to transition into homes of their own, to consider starting an OFF THE STREETS chapter in their own community. I thought that with such a clear vision, the process of getting to the goal would be straightforward and quick. I learned, however, that I had to be patient (and I am never patient). I learned that it wasn't I who was in charge, or Alice. It was the Holy Spirit.

> **Preach the Gospel, and if necessary use words.**
>
> **Often attributed to St. Francis of Assisi**

As the months passed, the Lancaster chapter started and began to thrive. OFF THE STREETS has learned a lot from that process. Then Deacon Kevin Moore contacted me from Bridgeport, Connecticut, and told me he wanted to start a chapter there. Soon after that we heard from Larry Burns and Bill Wright in Huntington Beach, California. Their success in starting a chapter of OTS without one face-to-face meeting with anyone from the East Coast is living proof that this ministry can be established and carried out anywhere. I am especially grateful to Joe Simons for creating the startup template that is being used for the first time in Huntington Beach. Joe has been key to the survival and growth of OFF THE STREETS and I am forever indebted to him.

If this book does indeed move you to make that initial inquiry, its purpose will be fulfilled, and I will be forever grateful to Alice for making it happen. (Her Afterword as well as the book's final pages, which I insisted she include, give further glimpses into who she is and what she does.)

I owe a tremendous debt of thanks to all the homeless and formerly homeless individuals who have courageously shared themselves and their stories at meetings about OTS, in videos, and in writing. Their willingness to speak has helped many eyes, minds, and hearts to see beyond the label *homeless*. To them I say, when you get to heaven, please look for me at one of the side entrances and sneak me in. God bless each of you!

Alice and I are both grateful to those who generously took time to read a draft of the manuscript and provide valuable feedback, including Fr. Cyrus Bartolome, Larry Burns, Thomas Carr, Don Cronauer, Andrew Curtin, Sandra Fluck, Fr. Joseph Gill, Dorothy Hayes, Deacon Peter Jupin, Fr. Michael Letteer, Mary Hendel McCafferty, Glenn McQuaig, Deacon Kevin Moore, Art Oles, Jack Oles, Vince Oles, Cari Raboin, Joe Simons, George Stadler, Donna Walker, and Bill Wright.

There is one more person I must thank, and she is the most important of all: my wife, Kathleen Oles. For many, many years she allowed me to spend time, energy, and money trying to figure out how I might help the homeless. If I was sacrificing, she too was sacrificing. Possibly her greatest contribution to OFF THE STREETS, however, came when we moved to Pennsylvania in 2012. When I said that I wanted to start and run an OFF THE STREETS chapter here, Kathleen put her foot down. "You'll do no such thing," she said. "You can have a kickoff meeting and show them what needs to be done—but you will not be running it!"

At first I was startled; she never speaks like this, in such a direct, absolute manner. I was shocked. It took a few days for me to realize what she was saying, and I came to believe that her words were inspired by the Holy Spirit. In essence what she was telling me was that if I ran OFF THE STREETS in Lancaster, that would probably be as far as it would go. It would have no future growth. I had to, as the saying goes, let go and let God. I did as the Spirit of God directed through my wife.

Additional Credits

Photo of Blessed Mother Teresa of Calcutta on page 6 by Alessia Giuliani, CNS News

Photo on page 9 by H. Dominique Abed, from http://www.freepik.com /index.php?goto=41&idd=348651&url=aHR0cDovL3d3dy5zeGMGMua HUvcGhvdG8vMTE3NjcoMQ==

Photo on page 10 from http://www.edupics.com/photo-homeless-i7897.html

Drawing on page 12 by Rembrandt van Rijn, "The Healing of the Blind Man of Jericho, c. 1659, from https://upload.wikimedia.org/wikipedia /commons/0/03/Rembrandt_224.jpg

Drawing on page 16 by Rembrandt van Rijn, "Jesus rettet den sink-enden Petrus," by Rembrandt, c. 1632/33, from http://www. sander-gaiser.de/ru/bilder/juenger/b2-31.jpg

Photo on page 18, NASA 11 liftoff, from http://history.nasa.gov/ap11ann /kippsphotos/39961.jpg

Painting on page 26, "Healing of a Blind Man," by Brian Jekel, from http://brianjekelfineart.com/gallery:14822/show/id:15188

Photo of Mike Kusen on pages 29 and 33 by Michael Duffy, Danbury News-Times

Photo on page 34 from http://www.freeimages.com/profile/eastop

Photo on page 42 by Andy Hall, The Guardian, from http://www.the guardian.com/world/gallery/2012/jun/16/andy-hall-greece

Photo on page 48 from Goodwill of Western and Northern Connecticut

Photo on page 80 by Donna Walker, Lancaster Online

Photo on page 92 by Steve Schapiro, http://www.steveschapiro.com

HOMELESS JESUS

"SON OF MAN HAS NO PLACE TO LAY HIS HEAD" MATTHEW 8:20

A November 11, 2013 article on the website of the official Vatican news network (http://www.news.va/en/news/homeless-jesus-sculpture-presented-to-pope-francis) reported that Canadian sculptor Timothy Schmalz had just presented to Pope Francis a sculpture depicting Jesus as a homeless man sleeping on a park bench. In an interview with Vatican Radio, Mr. Schmalz told reporter Philippa Hitchen, "My hope is to have in most of the big cities this visual message . . . so that people will have more concern about the homeless." It is the hope of Deacon Michael Oles, founder of OFF THE STREETS, for there to one day be a chapter of OFF THE STREETS in every community. It seemed fitting to pair the statue with this book. OFF THE STREETS is grateful to Mr. Schmalz for allowing us to use a photo of his sculpture in the book. Copies of the statue are available through the artist's website:

www.sculpturebytps.com

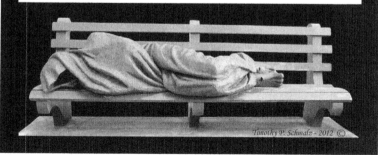

Timothy P. Schmalz - 2012 ©

Also produced by

Not Forgotten Publishing Services

Born Again in Medjugorje: A Memoir
by Mary Hendel McCafferty, June 2012

The Quarry: A Novel by Robert Carson, July 2012

*Nan & Clete . . . and Then There Was One:
Finding a New Normal After a Traumatic Death*
by Nancy S. Gibble, February 2013

Forget Me Not: A Tough and Tender Memoir
by Loraine Seavey Nixon Martin, March 2013

In God's Mercy: My Spiritual Journey
by Linda Lint, May 2013

The Little Society of St. Rita Prayer Book
by The Little Society of St. Rita, July 2013

*The Notebooks of the Reverend
Damien Marie Saintourens, OP*
by the Cloistered Dominican Nuns of the Perpetual Rosary,
Lancaster, PA, October 2013

Not.Forgotten.Publishing@gmail.com

From Bins to Book

"I tried everything, from buying 'how to write' books and audio-to-text converters to just sitting at the computer and typing for hours on end. What I ended up with was three plastic bins full of documents and references, hours and hours of audio files, and a boatload of Word files. I was drowning in my own drivel, clueless as to how to proceed. . . . Then one day . . . I heard about Alice Morrow Rowan of Not Forgotten Publications. . . . I will be forever grateful to Alice for making it happen."

Deacon Michael J. Oles, pages 120–121, Help the Homeless
OFF THE STREETS One Person at a Time

Afterthought

JUST ONE WEEK before this book was published, a checking account that my wife and I share was raided by a hacker who sent our balance into negative numbers. When we confronted the bank about what had happened, we were told it could take up to 90 days for them to "research" the matter. Meanwhile, we'd have to wait—with *no* certainty that we'd get our money back.

The money in that account, while significant, is not all we possess, but it *could* have been, and in the early years of our marriage it *would* have been. I recall how in 1984, when I retired from the Air Force, a financial planner offered to help Kathy and me. We invited him to meet with us in our home. As we talked, he learned that we had no savings or investments and were literally living paycheck to paycheck. He was shocked and couldn't understand why we had agreed to talk with him. I told him I'd had the impression he was going to help us figure out how to pay our bills!

A 2014 survey conducted by the American Payroll Association shows that more than two-thirds of Americans are now living paycheck to paycheck. This means that this many Americans would have no cushion to fall back on if what happened to us, or something similar, happened to them. They would not be able to pay their rent or mortgage and other expenses. Without help, they could quickly become homeless.

Homelessness—it's not so far-fetched. Many of us, me included, when we really examine why we're able to afford a life in our own home, will recognize that we had lots of help. OFF THE STREETS is a tried and true way that we can "pay forward" the help that we have received.

Please join us!

Made in the USA
Middletown, DE
24 December 2021

56853524R00076